PLAYING

WITH

MYSELF

PLAYING
WITH
MYSELF

Randy Rainbow

ST. MARTIN'S PRESS
NEW YORK

First published in the United States by
St. Martin's Press, an imprint of St. Martin's Publishing Group

www.stmartins.com

Designed by Devan Norman

Library of Congress Cataloging-in-Publication Data

Names: Rainbow, Randy, 1981- author.
Title: Playing with myself / Randy Rainbow.
Description: First edition. | New York : St. Martin's Press, 2022. |
Identifiers: LCCN 2021057158 | ISBN 9781250276254 (hardcover) |
    ISBN 9781250284129 (signed edition) | ISBN 9781250276261 (ebook)
Subjects: LCSH: Rainbow, Randy, 1981- | Comedians—United
    States—Biography. | Singers—United States—Biography.
Classification: LCC PN2287.R2225 A3 2022 | DDC 792.702/8092
    [B]—dc23/eng/20211207
LC record available at https://lccn.loc.gov/2021057158

Our books may be purchased in bulk for promotional, educational, or
business use. Please contact your local bookseller or the Macmillan
Corporate and Premium Sales Department at 1-800-221-7945, extension
5442, or by email at MacmillanSpecialMarkets@macmillan.com.

First Edition: 2022

10 9 8 7 6 5 4 3 2 1

For my mom, Gwen,
and all the women who've lifted and inspired me

Contents

1

Yes, It's My Real Name, Shut Up

It was the best of times, it was the worst of times. . . .

Fine, I didn't write that. But it's how I really wanted the opening chapter of this book to begin. No phrase could more perfectly epitomize the last six years of my life, full of unimaginable highs and lows, for me personally and on the world stage. Unfortunately, my buzzkill editor has advised against direct plagiarism. Apparently Mr. Dickens would be none too thrilled. And you know Charles . . . Gurl is litigious.

Of course it wouldn't be the first time I borrowed from one of the greats to create my own art. If you're reading this now, it's likely you've seen my song parody videos on the internet. It's more than likely at least one of them has popped up on your social media feed, or in an email from your favorite aunt at some point over the last few years. Perhaps you were so inclined to share one of them with your friends from work, or your boyfriend, or his mom, or your cool pansexual cousin, or that other aunt who's hopelessly devoted to Fox News but still has a commendable sense of humor and hard-core loves the score from *Les Mis.*

Or perhaps it wasn't your vibe and you rolled your eyes after the first few seconds before dramatically untagging yourself from the post in protest and returning to your preferred guilty internet pleasure: potato-scratching ASMR makeup tutorials (or whatever you're into). The point is, we're together now and I forgive you!

• • • • •

Yes, it's me! Randy Rainbow, or as many of you have inaccurately referred to me on various occasions throughout the years, "Rainbow Randy," "Robbie Raincloud," "Reading Rainbow," "Ryan Reynolds," and "oh, *that* queen."

Of course, there's also a fair-to-middling chance you have no idea who the hell I am (fame can be fickle like that these days). Perhaps I just looked too unbearably adorable on the jacket of this book for you to resist when you found it on the shelf at your local thrift shop or next to a pair of hideous Ivanka Trump made-in-China flats on the clearance rack at Nordstrom. Well, assuming you decided to throw caution to the wind and buy the book instead of those flats (which wouldn't have gone with anything in your closet anyway), please rest assured, I am extremely famous.

When they first asked me to write a whole book, I was hesitant. Sure, I'd already done a lot of autobiographical writing in my day, but mostly on Twitter. And after careful research, I determined that books often require more than 240 characters. "Fuck that," I concluded. (See what I did there?) I know, you're probably rolling your eyes and thinking, "Get a load of her, turning down book deals in this economy . . . ," and you're right.

Then I realized what a golden opportunity this could be, having now reached a certain level of maturity, to finally come out! Not in the way I came out to my best girlfriend Kelly in a hotel bathroom at the Tampa Marriott during the Florida State Thespians competition of 1999. When I say "come out," I mean more like in the "eighteenth-century aristocratic debutante presenting herself to society" kind of coming out. I never had a proper bar mitzvah because I dropped out of Hebrew school. And I never had a quinceañera like many of my friends because when I turned fifteen, my mother insisted I was not a young woman of Latin American heritage. So let's think of this book as a combo of all those time-honored, coming-of-age traditions I missed out on (minus the shitty DJ and plastic party favors).

See, if you're familiar with my work, you are likely familiar with my persona—the heightened-reality, campy, scripted, comedic version who often breaks into song. Sure, that's one part of me, but what you may not realize is that behind that bubbly character is an actual person—an introverted only child, full of angst, flaws, insecurities, past heartbreaks, and yes, impossibly perfect bone structure. Hopefully, as you read on, you'll come to know more about the person behind the persona behind the pink cat-eye glasses. But why not, let's kick right off by dispelling some of the most egregious "fake news," alternative facts, lies, myths, and propaganda often circulating about me.

1. It was once written in a review of my work that I am the love child of Harvey Fierstein, Bette Midler, and Anderson Cooper. While I was not able to fully corroborate this genealogy on Ancestry.com, nor can I practically imagine such a romantic tryst among those three gay icons (actually, now I'm totally imagining it, and so are you), I'm gonna go ahead and say that one's true. (Hey, it's my book.)

2. I've seen a number of QAnon-style conspiracy theories about me perpetuated by cyborgs, trolls, and bots on social media.

Recently, one such tweet referring to me as a "little mutant freak" claimed that I am "a CIA asset, probably born in a lab somewhere." This is also entirely true.

3. Some extreme right-wingers seem to believe I've been hired by Nancy Pelosi and the DNC to push their agenda. Joking aside, this is false. Believe it or not, my work is not at all politically motivated and neither am I. I've never been a political junkie by nature, and I'm not a pundit. My "shtick" as a topical comedian and satirist has always been to cover whatever *you, the audience,* are talking about. It just so happened that around 2016, y'all started talking about nothing *but* politics (I wonder why . . .), and I simply followed suit! While, like many, I have become much more woke to those topics over the years, and while some of my spoofs may contain a heavier dose of my genuine opinion than others, my work is rarely a personal testimony, and never a political endorsement, or even condemnation, in any grown-up sense of those words. It's merely a colorful snapshot of a moment in time as I see it, a funhouse mirror reflection of *all* sides. That has at least been my intention to this point, anyway. So don't act so surprised when you tell me your Republican mother loves me, too. I'm not. Why the hell shouldn't she?

4. Yes, it's my real name. "Randy Rainbow" (not Randall, not Randolph, not Randoncé) is the name that appears on my birth certificate, my New York State ID, my Social Security card, and in black Sharpie ink on the inside of every pair of underwear I own. I know, it sounds like the corniest stage name ever. Believe me when I tell you, I would not have chosen it for myself. It was a very difficult childhood

(just read the next few chapters!). My name may seem perfectly on-brand now, but frankly, that's only because I had no choice but to grow into it! For all those birthers out there still demanding receipts, here, once and for all, in plain black and white, in the very first chapter of my very own book, is everything I presently know about the official origin of my very real last name.

My great-great-grandparents, the Regenbogens, lived in what was then Austria-Hungary—likely between 1860 and 1880. Like many other Jews, they fled to England to avoid religious persecution. The German word *regenbogen* was literally translated to the English word "rainbow." The freshly minted Rainbow family became domestic servants in Great Britain (it's believed they served royalty and were somehow well known and highly regarded). Around 1900, they immigrated to the U.S., and since their name was already anglicized, no changes were made. Had they arrived as the Regenbogen family, it probably would have been changed to something like Rabinowitz, and I might quite possibly be an accountant today.

There you have it, folks! The explanation you've all been clamoring for. I'm sorry it didn't include unicorns or Judy Garland like I'm sure you anticipated. Trust me, I was disappointed about that myself. Of course, this long-standing mystery still begs the question as to why—knowing what a cruel world they were bringing their child into—my parents went right for the double-R alliteration and named me Randy. Sure, the kids on the playground still would have tormented me had I been John Rainbow or Adam Rainbow, but at least my name might have made me sound a little less like a cheap drag queen or the title character on a public access children's show when my elementary school teachers shouted it out during roll call. Well, the answer to that question is quite simple: My parents hated me. (I'm only half joking.)

● ● ● ● ●

So now that I've formally introduced myself and my forefathers, without further ado, here's the rest of my story so far. Some parts will be funny, some might be sad, and some will hopefully inspire you to follow your dream, call your mother, or maybe just stay home and play with yourself. It's not the entire story, mind you. This isn't a completely comprehensive memoir (I haven't quite reached Michelle Obama status yet). It's merely a colorful snapshot of a few moments in time as I've seen them, starting at the beginning-ish and following my wild ride down an unconventional path, through an unprecedented time, and right here to you.

Please silence your cell phones, refrain from flash photography, sit back, relax, and enjoy. The role of Randy Rainbow in this book will be played by—you guessed it—Randy Rainbow. And yes . . . that is his real name.

2

Pajama Bottoms

It was a balmy Saturday afternoon in mid-July of 1989. I had just celebrated my eighth birthday, but I didn't look a day over six and a half. While most of the other little boys on Long Island were at the park playing sports, splashing around the local swimming pool, or immersed in a spirited game of Double Dragon or similar form of virtual manslaughter down at the neighborhood arcade, I was in my bedroom on the second floor of our house on Larkfield Road in Commack tying pink ribbons into my hair and being fitted for a skirt.

The smell of baked apples and cinnamon wafted up from the kitchen. My mother had made themed snacks for the guests who would be arriving soon. I had decided a week prior to put on a major production of *Snow White and the Seven Dwarfs*, and it was at last opening day! My friends, who I'd cast in the roles of the dwarfs, forest creatures, and various other supporting tracks, were on their way over with their parents (the audience). I, naturally, would be making my big backyard debut in the title role of Snow White.

I stood in the middle of my room like Scarlett O'Hara being corseted up for the Twelve Oaks barbecue, my mother on the floor behind me, cutting the yellow sheet tied around my waist from the bottom to just above my ankles. I had recently learned to sew and had trimmed the sleeves of the white T-shirt I was wearing with lace. Layered on top of that was a blue tank top which served as a makeshift bodice.

Over my bed hung an official *Dirty Dancing* movie poster featuring Patrick Swayze as Johnny Castle, sprawled out on a floor, wearing a fitted black tank, matching pleather pants, and a come-hither "Hungry Eyes" look on his face. Thumbtacked to the adjacent wall was a life-sized, seventy-four-inch-long poster of Mikhail Baryshnikov in a distressed fishnet crop top and white ballet tights, lunging into fourth position. I had been taking dance lessons for two years, so all these images of chiseled abdomens and pronounced bulges adorning the walls seemed appropriate enough at the time. In retrospect, my eight-year-old childhood bedroom looked more like the men's room at a gay bar in Hell's Kitchen. There was even a giant rainbow decal stretching the length of the wall opposite my bed (obviously a nod to my surname, just in case being made fun of by dozens of children at school on a daily basis wasn't serving as enough of a reminder). It was not the conventional decor of most third-grade boys. All that was missing was a sign on the door saying TWO FOR ONE HAPPY HOUR.

The gold and orange Fisher-Price Record Player on the dresser was spinning the cast album of Disney's *Snow White Live at Radio City Music Hall*. The 1979 production, based on the animated feature, had been filmed and broadcast on HBO throughout the '80s. Our VHS copy had become one of my earliest and deepest obsessions. The full-scale, Broadway-style spectacle, which inspired the pop-up matinee about to take place on Larkfield Road, has since been credited with single-handedly reviving Radio City, which, just one year earlier, was preparing to close its doors forever and become a shopping center. If you love the Radio City Christmas Spectacular, you have *Snow White Live* to thank. (Fun Fact: Charles Edward Hall, who played the Wicked Witch in *Snow White Live*, is still playing Santa Claus in the Christmas show to this day!) I have since personally credited the televised event with single-handedly sparking my interest in and eventual intense passion for musical theatre.

The apples were all baked, my lewk was flawless, and the crowd was now seated and waiting for a show. I grabbed a black garbage bag filled with costume pieces and props, ran down through the kitchen and out the back door leading to the yard. My zealous emergence in costume was greeted with a generally positive, albeit hesitant mix of nervous laughter, "oohs and ahs," and applause. I was in heaven. A star was born.

I brought the garbage bag over to my friends who were now clustered upstage (on the grass) in front of what I guess you'd call the orchestra section of our concrete patio. As I carefully instructed each kid on which piece to take from the bag, I heard my friend Courtney quietly protest, witch's hat and bunny ears in hand, that *she* should play Snow White because *she* was the only "real girl" in our group. "Sorry, bitch," I thought as I pretended not to hear her. "This is my big break."

For the next sixty minutes or so, with no intermission, I ran around our backyard in full drag, giving a leading lady tour de force while simultaneously shouting stage directions at my costars who were by now terrified of me. It's exactly how I imagine Barbra Streisand must have looked on the set of *Yentl*.

During a recent home video viewing of that performance, as research for this book, what struck me most were all the parents—even the macho dads in their Yankees baseball caps and '80s porn mustaches—standing and clapping as we took our final bows. I don't know what they were thinking, or what the conversations were in their cars on the way home, but for 1989, this was certainly what you'd call a progressive audience.

Though Snow White had thus far been my most public presentation of its kind, I was no novice in this sort of gender-bending folly. From the age of two, my mother had put me to sleep with Broadway cast albums and the soundtracks to movies like *Oklahoma!* and *The Music Man*. A big fan of musicals, Mom was often singing around the house and introducing me to the classics. As the result of all this nurturing of my show queen gene, as it were, I was totally captivated by the genre, and particularly the women in it—how they sang, how they moved, how they dressed, and, of course, how they wore their hair. In my earliest years, you'd have been hard-pressed on any given day not to find little me in front of a television, fastidiously mimicking scenes from *The Wizard of Oz* or *Grease* as they played before me. I wanted so badly to live inside of those worlds. I vividly remember feeling physical pain knowing that I could never feasibly crawl into the TV and play on the other side of the screen.

Because the female lead was always my avatar of choice, I would wear a pair of yellow pajama bottoms on my head to emulate her long hair. This became rather habitual, and before long I was whippin' my pajama hair back and forth almost full-time around the house, along with other memorabilia from that day's performance. On *Mary Poppins* days, for example, I would carry an umbrella and one of my mother's makeup compacts everywhere I went, powdering my nose and chin the way Julie Andrews did in the opening title sequence. (The bud of what would eventually blossom into a serious Sephora addiction.)

Though I would come to find out in my adult years that some of the men in our family found my behavior concerning, I don't remember ever feeling it was discouraged. Maybe I just didn't notice if it was. Even my father, who would later claim to be completely blindsided by my coming out (more on that later), hot glued me a pair of my very own Ruby Slippers when I asked for them one Hanukkah. (Just as an aside . . . I hate to steal the crown and have armies of gay writers trolling me on Twitter, but could I—Randy Rainbow—be the gayest person in history ever to write a book? Discuss amongst yourselves.)

One thing I knew for sure was that we were a showbiz-positive family. There were tons of musicians on both parents' sides. My father, like my mother's father, had been a musician (drummer), singer, and bandleader most of his life. My great-grandmother Estelle performed in Yiddish theatre and later worked the borscht belt as a singer and actress. And though my mother never pursued it professionally beyond her star turn as Anna in a high school production of *The King and I*, she's always been a performer at heart. The story goes that in her youth, she'd pray every night before going to sleep that God would turn her into Bernadette Peters. (While that wish was never *technically* granted, she did eventually give birth to me, which I guess says something for the power of prayer.) The point is, performing arts were encouraged and celebrated, and I was never coerced or even cajoled to pick up a football, which I must say is only fair. I mean, you can't fucking name your kid Randy Rainbow and then expect him to be a star quarterback—or whatever they're called.

The second my feet started moving to the rhythm of the radio, there was a trip to Capezio, where I was fitted for jazz shoes. At age five, I was taken to a production of *The Nutcracker*. I began to cry during the finale, a ritual that became commonplace for me at every movie and live theatre event. I sobbed hysterically at the end of everything like I was being kidnapped. I always hated for fantasies to end. Still do.

It was more than that, though. I was overcome by the experience. The music and movement and emotion combined made it feel like my stomach was going up into my throat and coming out my ears. It was exhilarating. I was overstimulated, and my little body didn't know where to put all the feelings. I was also exasperated—all right, I was pissed off—by the fact that I was not up on the stage or screen participating myself.

"Do you wanna do that?" my mother asked as I wept.

"Yes!" I wailed, red-faced and snotty.

By the same time a year later, I was a bona fide ballet boy at the Huntington Ballet Theatre, and one year after that, starring as Fritz, the bratty little brother of the main protagonist, Clara, in their production of *The Nutcracker*. I of course would have preferred the lead (Clara), but in this version, Fritz accompanied his sister throughout the entire show, all the way to the Land of Sweets, where he even got a fierce pirouette solo, so I accepted the role.

All this championing of flamboyant self-expression and pajama hair extensions at home was great for me creatively, but did me no favors when it came time to venture into the real world. I was not prepared for the schoolyard bullies waiting for me there. I remember one day, in first grade, taking one of my mother's purses ("pocketbook" if you're on Long Island in the '80s . . . or "pock-a-book" as I always thought it was called because of our thick Long Island accents) to school with me. I don't know what compelled me to accessorize so boldly that day. I guess I thought the outfit needed it. I was instantly met with resistance from one of the other little boys in my class.

"Why do you have a giiiiirl bag? That's for girls!"

"What are you talking about?" I squeaked out timidly, startled by this goddamn inquisition. "It's not a girl bag . . . it's just . . . it's just a regular bag . . ." (It was most certainly a girl bag.) "You know . . . it's just a bag . . . for holding stuff."

I was doing my best to sell it in the moment but was caught off guard. I never imagined I'd have to defend this.

"Oh yeah?" he challenged. "What kinda stuff?"

I was trapped. The answer to his question was "nail polish and my

Mary Poppins makeup compact" and no way in hell was I about to divulge that information. In lieu of a witty retort, I burst into tears.

As the bullies grew larger, so did their vocabulary of names for me, and boys like me. I learned quickly to keep to myself and tried to blend in with the wallpaper or playground equipment as much as possible when at school. But somehow the other boys were still always moths to my flame. It was as if they could just smell something different about me (perhaps it was my Coco Chanel Eau de Parfum). At recess, they'd come in gangs to taunt me and name-call. I was never quick with a comeback, and to this day have always had trouble finding my words when faced with confrontation. All my emotions rush to the surface at once, everything goes white, and all verbal skills completely freeze up. There was nothing I could do but stand there and take it.

"Write it down," my mother coached me after a particularly harrowing school day. "Write down everything you want to tell those idiots, and this way, when it happens again, you'll know what you want to say. And even if you never say it, you'll at least get it out of your own head."

I took her advice and started transcribing everything I felt onto color-coded index cards. In the safety of my own bedroom, the words just poured out of me. Why couldn't I be this prolific in the moment???

The next day on the playground, when the other boys started in on me, I whipped out my multicolored notes and launched a formal counterargument. To my surprise and delight, they all listened intently to my anti-bullying address, politely applauded when I was through, and never bothered me again. Just kidding! We were in elementary school. They called me "fag" and walked away laughing before I could finish.

While this new cue card system didn't make me any more popular at school, it did give me my first real appreciation for written language. I was overflowing with thoughts and feelings I often struggled to articulate. The ability to assign words to each of them, whether or not anyone ultimately heard those words, gave me a sense of control that felt freeing and empowering. It's one of the reasons I've always loved the lyrical language of musical theatre, and why I would have preferred to be born a character in a musical. Show tunes have a way of perfectly marrying words to thoughts and feelings, and bringing order to chaos in a way I've always craved in reality. When shit goes down in a musical, no one struggles with what to say. The words just pour out of them—with pithy rhymes and tons of vibrato, no less—and in a matter of minutes, everything yearning to be said in the moment is fully expressed, wrapped up neatly, and even celebrated with applause. Yes, please!

Cue cards or no, these types of confrontations regarding my unorthodox style and demeanor over the years led to crippling anxiety and many trips to the nurse's office with pretend head or tummy aches, hoping my mother or grandmother would come to my rescue. They also led to massive insecurity and a dimming of the light I was being made to feel was perhaps too bright for some people. The way I gestured or spoke might attract unwanted attention, so when I was at school or outside of what I considered a safe zone, I turned the light inward and became withdrawn, restricted, and silent. I watched the seconds tick by on school clocks, waiting for the moment I could run home to my costumes, movies, and cast albums—my happy place.

3

Playing with Myself

It was 1990. The Milli Vanilli lip-syncing scandal had just devastated the soul of our nation. I was nine years old, in the back seat of our '89 Chrysler New Yorker, accompanied by a motley crew of Cabbage Patch dolls, our jittery West Highland White Terrier, Sugar, who was clearly strung out on coke, and multiple brown packing boxes labeled PLAY-ROOM and RANDY CLOTHES. My face was glued to my Game Boy and the cassette tape of *The Little Mermaid* soundtrack was now roughly in its twenty-fourth rotation on the car stereo. It had been playing on a loop for the entire eighteen-hour road trip. My mother was up in the passenger seat, about to lose her shit.

"Can't we listen to something—"

"No," I interjected stoically, never taking my eyes off the Tetris pieces falling into place on the monochrome screen in my hand. Even in the throes of her *Mermaid*-induced torture, my mother couldn't help but extol the clever lyrics of Howard Ashman as they danced seamlessly over Alan Menken's incredibly catchy score.

"*'Hot-ta under the wa-ta!'* Ha! Who the hell thinks of that???"

We were on our way to the home state of Disney World, so my choice of music was fitting. This was not a vacation, though, and the Rainbow household had become anything but the happiest place on Earth.

My father, who had been doing very well running the East Coast distribution of a successful skin care line out of a warehouse on the ground level of our home in Commack, had been swindled into a bum deal (something he'd become notorious for doing) and sold the business. Soon we were strapped for cash, and my mother took a day job at an office in the neighborhood. My father, on to his next get-rich-quick scheme, was now using the home warehouse to sell some revolutionary 3D camera technology. As it turned out, the only successes he wound up having in 3D were the triple D's attached to the secretary he'd hired to come work for him during the day. My mother came home for lunch one afternoon and found them on the floor together.

"Never go home for lunch" would soon become my mother's motto. When she made the mistake of doing it again a month later, she walked through the front door to find our landlords sitting cross-armed and expressionless at the kitchen table. To her surprise, my father, who was in charge of depositing the rent check every month, had apparently not made a single payment in almost half a year.

I was *so* invested in school and ballet by then. All my friends were in New York. Regardless of my tantruming and waterworks, a few weeks later I was saying goodbye to everyone and everything I knew, rolling up my Patrick Swayze poster, and on the road heading for the Sunshine State.

As fate would have it, my grandmother on my mom's side—my Nanny—who was still living in New York, had recently bought this town house in South Florida. She'd planned to move into it herself after retiring from the hospital where she worked as a registrar, but in light of recent events, she suggested we take it instead.

The Chrysler that brought us there would soon be repossessed. My mother and I would walk outside one morning to drive to school a few months later and find it gone. My father had also stopped making car payments. But for now, he was behind the wheel, chauffeuring us past rows of palm trees down Flamingo Road, turning into a cul-de-sac and onto the driveway of our new home in Cooper City, Florida.

I stepped out onto the suspiciously clean blacktop and instantly observed how bizarrely uniform everything looked. All of the houses were painted a variety of the same four bright colors: coral, light pink, seafoam green, and yellow. It was super tacky, but not the Long Island super tacky to which I'd grown accustomed. It looked like the neighborhood in *Edward Scissorhands*. I also noticed there were tons of kids playing outside in the streets.

"We're in one of the best school districts in the state," my mother boasted, clutching the dog leash for dear life as Sugar dragged her behind him on a mad peeing spree.

But why would Nanny want to retire to a great school district in a complex full of rambunctious kids my age? We would later speculate that on her search to find a house for herself, she'd likely had my best interests in mind the whole time. Nanny always had my back.

Nanny's real name was Irene. I started calling her Nanny as a baby because I thought we were British (actually, I couldn't pronounce "Grandma"). She was Lucille Ball, Joan Rivers, Bea Arthur, Betty White, Don Rickles, Elaine Stritch, and Joy Behar rolled into one (and a little Cardi B, for the millennials and Gen Zs in the audience). No one on Earth was or has ever been funnier and I'll testify to that before Judge Judy herself. She didn't have to try, either. Humor just flowed naturally from her pores. It was part of her, like an appendage. And when she was on a roll, it was the most perfect symphony I'd ever heard. She was irreverent, self-deprecating, opinionated, savagely quick-witted, a Michelangelo of sarcasm, the greatest storyteller around (she made a twelve-course meal out of every anecdote), and had movie star good looks like Elizabeth Taylor. She spoke with a New York accent and cursed a lot but she was classy as fuck. (Nanny would have immediately followed that last sentence with, "Sorry, can I say 'classy'?" Her timing was off the charts.) The air truly changed when she walked into a room. Everything just got brighter. It was molecular.

She joined us in Florida shortly after we arrived, settling permanently into a more lifestyle-friendly condo complex nearby. Mom and Dad both started working full-time right away, so Nanny would pick me up every day after school and take me on excursions to the mall or Michaels craft supply—ya know, real wild and crazy shit.

Nanny had a heart of gold but definitely wasn't what you'd call an optimist. She was easily aggravated by almost everything and everyone, and wasn't afraid to tell you all about it. She even hated most of her friends (or at least acted as if she did) and had offensive, secret nicknames for them. I'd throw my backpack in the back seat of her car, climb into the passenger's side, and barely have time to close the door before she'd launch into her latest tirade about "Crazy Shirley," "Schmucky Susan," or her infuriating trip to the DMV. By the end, I'd often be choking from laughter. No matter the subject of her diatribe, she had this magical ability to immediately convert her negative energy into a hilarious performance piece, which then became a gift to the listener. It was from her I learned that anger not only *could* be funny, but *should* be funny—always.

If I have any sense of comedic timing, it comes largely from Nanny. She always had the TV on at her house, and would walk around talking back to it all day. If a celebrity or politician was being interviewed, she'd respond to the TV as though she were conducting the interview herself. I frequently notice myself mimicking a lot of her style and rhythm in my videos. I'm basically just an old lady talking back to her television set.

●　●　●　●　●

During the elementary school day, I was notably shy and antisocial. I never quite acclimated to my new surroundings and wasn't a natural when it came to bonding with classmates. I had seen kids on scripted television shows with imaginary friends and decided that might be a viable option to explore. For a while, I had a very serious relationship with a blue rubber dinosaur eraser I bought at a book fair. He was fun, but we ultimately decided to call it quits. I guess I rubbed him the wrong way. (GOOD NIGHT, I'LL BE HERE ALL WEEK!)

My awkward introversion followed me to middle school. I'd spend lunchtime in my own little corner of the cafeteria, doodling in note-books and watching other kids fraternize. For some reason, though, when it came time to audition for school plays, I was able to put my insecurities and timidity on hold, get in there, and get the job done. There wasn't a tryout sign-up sheet that didn't have my name on it, as intimidating as it may have felt for me to write it there. I guess all my early stage work, both in ballet and the backyard, gave me the chutzpah and a certain work ethic when it came to show business.

I had a nice singing voice for my age, so I landed the lead in all our school musicals. Perhaps you caught my triumphant performance as Father Time in the smash hit musical *Computerized Holidays*? Or maybe you recall my heartbreaking portrayal of the aging, lovelorn river pilot in *Steamboatin': A Musical Journey Down the Mississippi*? (I don't remember much about that show, but I'm pretty sure if you dug up a video of it, the entire class of 1991 at Pioneer Middle School would be canceled.)

Looking back, it must have seemed bizarre to the other kids in school. I mean, here I was, the weird little shy boy in the corner who was by all accounts completely mute, suddenly standing center stage at their afternoon assembly, belting out power ballads. This drastic dichotomy was paradoxical, even to me. All I knew was that it felt right, and when I was singing or performing both the kids and adults paid attention to me in a way they never had in real life. Onstage became the only place I felt truly seen.

Back at our house, I was trying to make myself as invisible as possible. The already tense relationship between my parents had only become more strained, which meant a lot of fighting. My father's rage led to intensely scary temper tantrums, which gave me nightmares every night. I started to become more and more reclusive in my own home. I'd lock myself in my room and lose myself in movies and music. Before long, I started bringing my dinner plate upstairs to avoid dreaded dinner table confrontations. Luckily, ever-advancing technology made it easier for me to occupy myself in solitary confinement. I now had my own CD player, and my collection of Broadway cast albums was growing rapidly. A new handheld Sony camcorder I'd gotten for my birthday inspired a series of stop-motion animation shorts starring my *Teenage Mutant Ninja Turtle* and *Beauty and the Beast* action figures. And let's be real: This was also right around the time I'd begun to discover the preadolescent wonders of masturbation, so let's just say I had my hands full with that.

●　●　●　●　●

My CD collection was not the only thing growing rapidly. As I became more isolated, having now broken up with all my rubber erasers, I moved on to a new pair of friends: pizza bagels and potato chips. Every day after school, while hiding in my room and hoping no one would notice me, I binged endlessly on junk food and started to rapidly put on weight. It seemed the smaller I tried to make myself, the bigger I got.

I spent every Friday night at Nanny's condo—a welcome vacation from the revival of *Who's Afraid of Virginia Woolf?* regularly going on at my parents' house. Nanny loved to spoil me, usually with food. At her house, I was "the king." She would set me up in front of the television in her bedroom with a folding snack tray over my lap.

"What would the king like for his supper?" she'd ask, holding an imaginary pen and pad in her hands, ready to take my order.

"Burger and fries," I'd say, delighted by her performance.

"The king wants a burger and fries!" she'd sing as she waltzed back into the kitchen. Nanny often joked about her infamously terrible singing voice, but she also had a way of singing everything. The best way I can think to describe it to you is that it sounded kind of like the singsong way Oprah would introduce guests on her talk show. *"John Travoooolta! Jennifer Aaaaaaniston! Burger and friiiiiies!"* That's pretty spot-on, actually.

Twenty minutes later, Nanny would return to her bedroom with my dinner plate in hand.

"One hamburger for the king! Here, let me fix your napkin and put ketchup on your fries for you. God forbid His Majesty should lift a damn finger!"

Even though she was pampering me, she was also most definitely roasting me. Nanny was an insult comic at heart.

• • • • •

Other than my wild weekend getaways to the Hollybrook Retirement Community, however, I did not have much of a social life. Mom took me to try out a local dance studio one afternoon. It had been recommended to us by my previous ballet instructor in New York, but I was quick to be unimpressed by the facility after one class. I was in the middle of dramatically Yelp-reviewing the experience to my mother as we were getting in the car to go home when she pulled a flyer from her

windshield. It was an advertisement for the Hollywood Playhouse, a lo-
cally beloved 1950s mainstage theatre that ran a summer and weekend
program for kids. One family orientation a week later and I was sold.
The Hollywood Playhouse would become my most magical safe haven
for the next several years, and my creative experiences there are some
of the most influential of my life.

We put on full-scale shows, often musical reviews written by the
staff using parodies or covers of existing theatre music. We had full
access to all the top-notch set pieces and costumes used for their adult
productions. This was the real deal. (So long, pajama bottoms!) While
the scripts they gave us were certainly age appropriate, they weren't
dumbed down, and were often filled with shades of adult humor and
double entendres—not like that hacky kid shit they were throwin' me in
elementary school! The instructors were all working performers, writers, musicians, and directors—true theatre folk, some with Broadway
credentials. It was the most valuable theatre education an eleven-year-
old in South Florida could wish for.

I quickly developed devastating crushes on every single boy I met
at the Hollywood Playhouse. More importantly, I made real friends
there—best friends, some of whom would remain my second family
for years to come: Bennie Lynn, Sami Rudnick, Vanessa Cohen, and
another little boy named Josh Gad. Josh and I got along famously, onstage and off. He made me belly laugh and I always returned the favor.
He used to get really invested in his characters and scene work. During
one scene he and I shared in an Irving Berlin revue called "Manhattan Magic," in which I played a Gene Kelly–type womanizer and Josh
played a high-strung, chain-smoking stage manager with a fixation on
his next-door neighbors' sex life (did I mention we were eleven?), I remember watching him really "go for it" in a way I'd never seen another
kid our age perform before.

"What a weirdo," I thought.

Some Saturdays after rehearsal, Josh and I would go back to one of our houses to make home movies, which often led to sleepovers full of late-night laugh fests. His bedroom was a shrine to Disney. The walls were covered with movie posters, collectable animation cels, a personally signed letter from Michael Eisner (then CEO of The Walt Disney Company), and framed Disney theme park maps.

"What a weirdo," I again thought.

Roughly two decades later, all that "weird" behavior would pay off when Josh would go on to be Tony nominated in the Best Leading Actor in a Musical category for *The Book of Mormon*, and shortly thereafter become a Disney icon himself, voicing the role of Olaf in *Frozen* (talk about mastering the art of visualization!).

I was inspired by Josh, even back then. Before long, my bedroom was also decorated like the Magic Kingdom. There was something infectious about his dedicated fanaticism. It was more than childish enthusiasm; it was a focused and driven passion. I had that in me, too. It just hadn't occurred to me until now to express it through interior design!

It also taught me a valuable life lesson: "Weird is good. Be weird."

4

Lip-Syncing for My Life

Between Friday date nights with Nanny and Saturdays with my friends at the Hollywood Playhouse, weekends were primo! The lion's share of time spent in between at home and in school was now my only problem.

Mom and I had a great time together in the afternoons, going to movies and for ice cream at the mall when she finished with work. But our house was ruled by my father's erratic mood swings, which often triggered bouts of sulking and verbal assaults on me and my mother (a symptom of what I now recognize was likely severe depression). My stomach would sink at the sound of his car pulling into the driveway. When he came through the door, the black cloud descended, and straight up to my fortress I fled, surrounded by a moat of Bagel Bites and Yoo-hoo.

It was around this time I was introduced to a form of religion that was new to me: Barbra Streisand. I came downstairs one morning before school and my mother launched into her gay agenda.

"*Funny Girl* was on TV last night. I taped it for you and ordered you the soundtrack because you're gonna want the soundtrack after you watch the movie."

"Okay," I said, passively complying.

She didn't even look up at me as she rummaged through her purse looking for car keys. It was as if she were a drill sergeant rattling off marching orders to her new recruit. From then on, much of my time upstairs was spent lip-syncing to songs from *Funny Girl* and *Hello, Dolly!*, or watching, with assiduous concentration, Barbra's television specials from the 1960s, *My Name Is Barbra* and *Color Me Barbra*. I had scored VHS copies of both on a recent New York trip to the Museum of Television & Radio in Manhattan. (We didn't have YouTube or Amazon when I was a kid. We had to take airplanes to other states and look for shit!)

It was around this same time I was also introduced to another form of religion: Cool Ranch Doritos. I was right at the pearly gates of puberty, and the additional weight gain was doing nothing for my self-confidence or popularity. Believe it or not, chubby, effeminate boys were not at the top of the middle school food chain back then. I suddenly became very uncomfortable in my clothes. Nothing fit right anymore. It was embarrassing. Luckily, I came up with what I thought was the perfect solution! I exclusively started wearing double-extra-large T-shirts covered with very bright, very busy pictures of cartoon characters, in an effort to hide and distract from my actual body underneath. Because what better way to avoid calling attention to my physique than to shroud it in excessive amounts of fabric camouflaged by giant, aggressively vibrant renderings of Mickey Mouse and the Tasmanian Devil?

This heavy rotation of gaudy casual wear sparked running jokes about my fashion sense from friends and family that would continue for years. I pretended to laugh them off, but inside I was panicking.

My lack of social interacting at school left me plenty of time alone with my imagination. I would often fantasize throughout the day that I was different characters from my favorite musicals. Not only did this help pass the time, it became something of a coping mechanism. It kind of allowed me to manage my social anxieties by romanticizing them into dramatic narratives and theatrical plot twists. While walking the hallways of the school building, surrounded by cliques of other students who most certainly did not understand me, I was Belle strolling through the village of her poor, provincial town in *Beauty and the Beast*. At lunchtime, I would sit alone in the back of the auditorium, pretending I was Christine Daaé in the audience of the Paris Opera House, hiding from the Phantom of the Opera. And when the final bell rang to release us for the day, I was Jean Valjean breaking his parole, and fleeing the troubled prison guard Javert in *Les Misérables*. (Okay, fine. I never pretended I was Jean Valjean. I just felt like I needed to throw in a boy character so you wouldn't judge me, but fuck it. Who am I trying to impress?)

I was sitting in seventh-grade English class one morning with Yosemite Sam all over my tits, waiting for the bell to ring.

"Don't forget your homework assignment for tonight," our teacher, Mr. Edwards, anxiously reminded us before the strike of noon.

"Ugh, I already did," I said in a throwaway monotone under my breath.

The broad shoulders I was staring at began to bob up and down. The boy seated in front of me was apparently amused by the dry delivery of my little aside. He turned around, still midchuckle, to catch a glimpse of the hilarious stand-up comedian who had just caught him off guard.

His name was Jason. We shared a few classes together, but until now, he'd never really acknowledged me. I always noticed him, though. He was very cute, and though I wouldn't fully come to terms with my sexuality for another five years or so, I knew there was something about this Jason. His hair was short and dark with lightly frosted tips (because the

'90s) and ever-so-slightly spiked up perfectly into a seemingly effortless coiffure. His features were chiseled and square and his teeth were exceptionally straight. While so many kids at that age (myself included) were still waiting for their heads to give birth to their actual faces, his already looked fully developed. His plain white V-neck T-shirt was fitted snugly to his slim, sculpted frame and didn't even require any Looney Tunes characters to cover anything up.

"You're funny," he said in a remarkably mature voice, roughly six octaves deeper than my own.

Well, that was that. I now knew the way to my man's heart and, trust me, I took full advantage of it. From then on, English class became Comedy freakin' Central, and honey, I was the main attraction. I was shooting off one-liners and sarcastic quips any chance I got, being rewarded every time with Jason's approval—I mean laughter. My act was usually only intended for an audience of one, but Jason soon started opening my fan club up to other members of our class.

"Yo, you guys, this kid is hilarious," he'd pitch to neighboring students when one of my wisecracks was just too funny for him to keep to himself. Though I'd normally been super quiet and reserved in this type of setting, I now started to break out of my shell a little, and it felt pretty good.

Before I knew it, Jason and I were teamed up for a creative class project on Shakespeare. We were instructed to choose our own partners. . . . He asked and I said yes!!!

"Remember, tomorrow is Spirit Day," said Mr. Edwards. "If you're wearing school colors, the extra-credit points will go toward your projects."

Jason whipped around in his desk and with playful authority said, "We're doin' it."

I clammed up a little. I was usually very rigid about my wardrobe routine and none of my regular four T-shirts were blue and red. Whatever, though! It was one stupid day and there was no way I was about to disappoint my new life partner—I mean project partner. I had Nanny drive me to Target after school. The only suitable option we could find was a light blue baseball shirt with red sleeves, and the only one left was a medium. I tugged at the thin cotton blend as I looked at myself in the fitting room mirror, trying to stretch it into a large. "Who cares," I reassured myself as I started to sweat a little (I definitely cared). "It's fine, and actually, I look pretty cute in this."

That night I fell asleep staring at the blue and red baseball shirt hanging from a knob on my closet door. I had ironed it meticulously, so it was perfectly uncreased and ready to go. Even though I knew I'd be stepping out of my comfort zone a bit, I had kind of worked myself up into a little excitement about the whole thing. Jason and I would get our points, and I had a cute new outfit. I even found a red baseball cap to accessorize it with (look who's suddenly into sports!).

My first three periods on Spirit Day went off without a hitch. I was rocking my new look and feeling surprisingly full of myself (though I did strategically hold my books over my stomach on walks between classes. Baby steps . . .). I'd never been one to exhibit an overwhelming sense of pride about any cockamamie school, but it did feel nice to participate, and I loved the idea that Jason and I were in this together. I couldn't wait to see him.

The fourth-period bell rang and I ran to English. I walked through the classroom door, headed for my desk to find Jason already seated in his blue T-shirt. He swung around, took one look at me, and said with a quiet giggle, "Oh my god, you really are fat."

My heart started racing. Everything went white.

"Shut up," I breezily clapped back, trying to sound as if he hadn't just knocked the wind out of me. For the next hour, Jason carried on as though nothing had happened. I don't think he realized that something had. I didn't make any jokes that day. We got the fucking points.

I got home from school that afternoon and did what any normal, red-blooded twelve-year-old boy would do under the circumstances: I threw the damn baseball shirt in the garbage, locked myself in my room, and lip-synced to "My Man" from the *Funny Girl* soundtrack for five hours.

• • • • •

A few weeks later, my mother and I took one of our road trips to visit my grandpa, her father. He and Nanny had divorced long before I came into the picture (you should've heard Nanny's nicknames for *him*) and he was now living in Pennsylvania with his new wife and son. I was very preoccupied with my latest fascination: the recently released Barbra Streisand retrospective box set called *Just for the Record*. It was four hours and seven minutes of greatest hits, rare live performances, demo recordings, award acceptance speeches, and other random treasures encased in a pink linen box with a shiny gold rose on the front. (If you don't own it, omg, what are you even doing here???)

I was downstairs in Grandpa's basement with my Discman listening to "A Good Man Is Hard to Find" from her 1967 special *The Belle of 14th Street*. I needed something to drink, so I headed upstairs to the kitchen. As I rounded the corner from the living room, I pulled my headphones off and overheard the adults deep in deliberation at the kitchen table. It sounded a little heated, so I slowed down before stopping in my tracks to listen in.

"It's fine," I heard my mother say, making her case to Grandpa. "I was the same at his age. He'll grow out of it."

Grandpa, a handsome, fit man who historically had a propensity for voicing harsh criticism of his daughter (also overweight as a child), didn't seem to be buying what she was selling now.

"Well, you better do something about it, Gwen. The kid's as big as a house."

Grandpa and I were never very close. I only saw him a couple of days at a time when we made the infrequent schlep to Pennsylvania, and there wasn't much between us. I was surprised to hear him taking even this much interest in me now. Years later, I'd learn that he'd always expressed concern to my mom that my "tendencies" might rub off on his new son, Richard, who was about my age. I guess he was paying more attention to me than I thought.

As my face flushed, I backed away from the kitchen, suddenly no longer thirsty, and ducked into the guest room where I'd been stationed. I locked the door behind me, put my headphones back on, plopped to the floor in front of a full-length mirror, and began to lip-sync to Barbra's 1969 Academy Awards acceptance speech.

> *Hello, gorgeous! Well, I'm very honored to be in such magnificent company as Katharine Hepburn. Gee whiz . . .*

I sat there rewinding and repeating manically for an hour until my performance was memorized and perfected. I didn't know how else to escape the moment. On the heels of my recent Jason catastrophe, this was too much. I didn't know who to talk to and couldn't have found the words to express myself anyway, so I borrowed Barbra's instead.

> *Hello, gorgeous! I'm very honored to . . .*
> *Hello, gorgeous! Well, I'm very honored to be in such . . .*
> *Hello, gorgeous!*
> *Hello, gorgeous!*
> *Hello, gorgeous!*

I was literally lip-syncing for my life.

5

You're a Gay Man, Charlie Brown

(or "A Funny Thing Happened on the Way to the Toilet")

"Yo, Charlie Brown!"

"What's up, Charlie Brown?!"

"Oh shit, it's Charlie Brown!"

Those are not titles of classic Peanuts holiday specials. They were the taunts and jeers that followed me through the hallways for most of my high school career.

I stayed pretty under the radar as a freshman. My parents moved us to another district after sixth grade, which put me in another new school for seventh and eighth. The shift from middle school to high school was yet another big change. The building was bigger and so were the bullies. Even the drama department, which was putting on a production of *Mame* that year, seemed much loftier and more sophisticated than anything I'd seen in school. Though I certainly felt seasoned enough to audition, my social anxiety got the better of me, so I decided to sit my first year out (and you *know* Mame is my dream role!). It wasn't until sophomore year that I finally hit my stride.

One Friday afternoon, my drama teacher, Mr. Kinder, put on a video for our class. It was the original Broadway production of Stephen Sondheim's *Sweeney Todd*, starring Angela Lansbury and George Hearn. I was spellbound within the first ten minutes.

"Hold the fucking phone," I thought to myself as the other kids in class used the time to socialize, completely disregarding and disrespecting the intensely dramatic VHS magnificence unwinding before us. "What in holy Hal Prince am I witnessing right now and how do I inject it into my veins?"

Talk about the perfect marriage of words and music! This was everything that appealed to me about the genre but on a whole new level. Every lyric was like someone completing a Rubik's Cube before my very eyes. It was flawless! And the insanely clever, absolutely immaculate rhymes?! I mean, "fop/shop/shepherd's pie peppered with actual shepherd on top"??? Get the fuck out of here!

By the following week, my cast album collection would be completely refurbished to include all of Sondheim's masterpieces—*Into the Woods, Company, Sunday in the Park with George,* and so on. I had long been indirectly aware of his earlier collaborative works like *Gypsy* and *West Side Story*, of course. And I knew of *Into the Woods* by name only because when I was six years old in New York, I saw the commercials for it every day and begged my parents to take me. (Against my wishes, they brought me to see *Cats* instead. I don't wanna talk about it.) But this afternoon viewing of *Sweeney Todd* in drama class was my first real introduction to one of his solo gems, and I was hypnotized. We were surrounded by a group of rowdy teens and yet there was no one in the room but me and that piece-of-shit 1996 Panasonic TV/ VCR combo.

The bell rang before the end of act 1. I stayed after and asked Mr. Kinder if I could bring the tape home with me to finish it over the weekend. Impressed by my interest, he obliged and also seized the opportunity to encourage me to audition for the drama department's upcoming production of *You're a Good Man, Charlie Brown*. (Apparently he saw something in the acting assignments I'd been doing in class.) I guess it was the formal invitation I'd been waiting for. A week later I worked up enough courage, along with sixteen bars of a song (the rarely remembered introductory verse of "Somewhere Over the Rainbow," not sung by Judy Garland in *The Wizard of Oz*). I auditioned and got the lead.

During my run in the show, and from then on, kids at school delighted in any chance to call me by new sobriquet. I couldn't walk from one class to another without hearing "Charlie Brown!" shouted at me by passersby. I could never decipher which of them were fans and which were just blatantly mocking me. I'm sure the latter had the majority, but of all the nicknames I'd come to know through my school years, this was a welcomed new addition. I was still pretty round, still wearing loud Mickey Mouse T-shirts, and by now had completed my look with a pair of thick, Coke-bottle prescription glasses. Let's face it: I got off easy with "Charlie Brown." And honestly, more than anything, I was proud to be acknowledged for my stage work.

This new recognition gave me a jolt of self-confidence. Soon, I started opening up more and more and eventually made my core group of high school friends: Matt, Evyan, Candie, and Kelly. Matt, the only other boy in our group—with his trim physique and classic, blond, pretty boy good looks—certainly left me feeling like "the funny one." I often overcompensated with humor, holding court at our cafeteria lunch table with experimental stand-up comedy routines and an ever-expanding list of celebrity impressions, from Gwen Stefani to Diana Ross.

I also succeeded over the next three years in making my mark on the drama club, starring in many of its major productions and taking home big prizes at district and state competition festivals. I had come into myself, and gurl, I was crushing! Academically, on the other hand, I was crashing. I was so possessed by the success and joy my work in the theatre department had brought me, I began skipping all other periods to work on concerts and showcases I was directing for my drama troupe, or to rehearse for the annual musical. I barely went to any real classes by the end of senior year, and had even skipped many of my final exams. . . .

• • • • •

Hold up! Should I even be writing this in a book? Are they gonna make *me*—a published author on *The New York Times* Best Seller list (I'm assuming)—go to summer school or something now??? What's the statute of limitations on this stuff???

• • • • •

Anyway, there's really no logical justification for how I actually graduated from high school, except the faculty's appreciation for my musical chops. One afternoon, I made a rare appearance in my science class, just to show face. I barely remembered which desk was mine, and realizing how behind I was, had a full-on panic attack during the lesson. Toward the end of class, as we were all packing up, my teacher, Mrs. O'Grady, began walking directly toward me.

"Oh, shit," I thought. "She's gonna ask where I've been. She's gonna ask where all my missing assignments are and I won't have an answer. This is it. I'm dead."

She placed her hand on my desk, knelt down to meet me at eye level, and whispered, "I just loved you in *Guys and Dolls*."

Phew! Luck be O'Grady tonight!

• • • • •

Meanwhile, things at home were still a hot mess. It seemed the more I grew into myself and the more confidence I found, the more my father began to resent me. At the time, I was too naive to recognize it as resentment. Nanny would sometimes mention nonchalantly that he was jealous of me, but that didn't register. To this day it seems almost an inconceivable dynamic between parent and child. I was a kid. I was *his* kid. What was there to resent? But the truth was, he was unfulfilled in his life and unhappy with himself. He *was* jealous—jealous of my youth and future, and he really started to make it known. I began to feel like an uninvited foreign exchange student in my own house.

For me, prime time at home was in the afternoon—those few hours after school, before my parents got home from work. There was no yelling, no fighting, no withering side glances from my father . . . just me and Rosie O'Donnell. I ran home every day to catch *The Rosie O'Donnell Show*—the hottest thing in daytime television back then. I was beyond obsessed. Rosie was from Commack, New York, just like me. She had the same Long Island accent as my mom and much of my family, and many of the same insidery theatrical sensibilities as my friends from the Hollywood Playhouse. She was infatuated with Barbra Streisand and all things Broadway. I don't care what anyone says, *The Rosie O'Donnell Show* was being produced five times a week exclusively for me, and me alone. (I'm sure many people felt the same.)

There were no digital video recording systems back then, so I taped every episode on VHS (fuck, I'm old), most importantly to catch any Broadway performances that might be featured that day. I sat enraptured on the rose-colored leather couch in our Florida living room from

3:00 to 4:00 P.M. Eastern, devouring every moment with my eyeballs. I just wanted to live inside that show, on the shiny set at Rockefeller Center. I wanted to be in New York City, where Broadway was, and where all those performers lived! I'd lie back and gaze out the sliding-glass doors to our backyard, up into the goddamn sunny sky, past all those goddamn palm trees, and have imaginary conversations with Rosie.

"Wasn't Rebecca Luker amazing on the show today?" I'd ask her.

"Amazing," she'd concur. "*Sound of Music* revival tonight? I have tickets."

"Wouldn't miss it," I'd say. "Sardi's before?"

"Meet you at six!"

I wanted to be her friend. Why wasn't I her fucking friend???

It was around this time my mother and I began taking summer trips to New York with my friend Vanessa and her mother, Laurie, who had become a best friend to my mom and a second mom to me. This long-standing tradition gave me some of my most cherished theatre memories, like seeing the original cast of *Rent* for the first time (and subsequently second, third, and eventually forty-eighth times), Julie Andrews in *Victor/Victoria*, Betty Buckley in *Sunset Boulevard*, Alan Cumming in *Cabaret*, Bebe Neuwirth and Ann Reinking in *Chicago* . . . (damn, I miss the '90s!). These annual excursions became my lifeline throughout the year, but just weren't enough to truly satisfy my New York state of mind.

By now, my bedroom had graduated from Mickey Mouse to Manhattan. My friend Evyan, a skilled artist with a shared passion for Broadway and Barbra (thanks to my good influence . . . yes, Evyan, I'm taking full credit), came over one weekend and painted a mural of the New York City skyline that wrapped around my entire room. Above the black silhouetted buildings with their little yellow windows, we painted a night-blue sky and hung Broadway show posters, autographed programs I'd collected from dozens of stage doors, and pictures of all the performers we worshipped: Bernadette Peters, Patti LuPone, Linda Eder, Billy Porter, Sam Harris, Audra McDonald . . . My bedroom looked like a cheap bagel joint in Times Square. It was magnificent.

The doors to my closet were reserved for computer printouts and magazine clippings of comedy idols and stars of the silver screen like Judy Garland, Lucille Ball, Steve Martin, Martin Short, Dick Van Dyke, and Carol Burnett, as well as iconic composers like Stephen Sondheim, Andrew Lloyd Webber, Stephen Schwartz, and Alan Menken. I had made my bedroom—my sanctuary—a shrine to all the people and things in show business I loved and that inspired me. I wouldn't realize until later in life that I had also, somewhat unwittingly, built myself a personal vision board of sorts.

・・・・・

While my parents fought down on the first floor, I was locked upstairs in my cheap bagel joint, learning the choreography I taped on Rosie that day and acting out full, one-man productions of Broadway shows to the accompaniment of my cast recordings. By now, I had an encyclopedic knowledge of every musical in my stash—*Damn Yankees, Kiss of the Spider Woman, Jekyll & Hyde, Once on This Island* . . . I'd study and mimic every nuance and inflection I heard in every lyric, line delivery, and harmony (working diligently on my falsetto so I could nail all the girl parts, too).

Inspired by episodes of MTV's *Making the Video*, I was also starting to dabble in video production. I'd put on god-awful Halloween wigs, turn our cheap camcorder on myself—selfie style—and re-create my favorite pop music videos, like Britney Spears's "Oops! . . . I Did It Again" and Mariah Carey's "Heartbreaker." I had no access to editing software back then (what teenager did?), so I had to build each video, shot by shot, until it was complete. I would hit record, lip-sync to a few seconds of the song, hit stop, rewind and check the tape to make sure the timing was right, set up a new shot, hit record, lip-sync, stop, and so on. I didn't even have a way to lay audio over video back then, so for playback, I had to sync up the video with the actual music track on CD (like the silent movie system of the 1920s), which usually took about half a dozen tries. It was maddening and sometimes took days to perfect, but well worth it. My DIY pop music homages wound up being big hits with my friends, who'd come over and demand to watch them on repeat. (Where was YouTube when I needed her?!)

My father, on the other hand, who was pushing me to get serious about a career path, was less enthusiastic.

"You're never gonna earn a living wearing wigs and making silly videos on your camcorder," he'd say.

Whatever, gurl.

● ● ● ● ●

Okay, now that we've reached this point in my book, I know what you're probably thinking. You're probably thinking: "Look, I'm not one to stereotype anyone based on their musical tastes or the pajama pants they wore on their heads as children, but if I were forced to draw my own conclusions about this Randy Rainbow's sexual identity, based solely on the information relayed to me thus far, it might not be off base of me to take a stab in the dark and venture to guess that perhaps he may not be a heterosexual."

Hey, I'm totally with you! It seems fairly evident to me, as I write about it. Believe it or not, though, for a large majority of the people in my life, it still had not seemed to click. And to complicate matters even more, in the time-honored tradition of young gay men and their besties, while I was secretly lusting after the hot guy playing Kenickie in our school production of *Grease*, many of my gal pals seemed to be developing crushes on me. (Apparently, I was a much sexier Charlie Brown than I realized.) Even my best buddy and own bedroom Picasso,

Evyan, had acquired a little puppy love for me. When her romantic overtures were not reciprocated, her frustration culminated in a dramatic display at our State Thespian competition.

We students were all assigned rooms on the same floor of the hotel in Tampa where the competition was held. It always wound up a very communal situation, despite chaperones' efforts to keep us separated. I was leaving my room late one afternoon to meet my group for dinner before that evening's closing ceremony. Halfway to the elevator I realized I'd forgotten to pee, and noticing a door to one of the other rooms left ajar, knocked to no response and helped myself to the bathroom. I was washing up when suddenly I heard the lock click on the front door of the room. A small crowd from our troupe, led by Evyan, already mid-rant, entered and walked past the sliding bathroom door, which was only slightly cracked, not realizing there was someone on the other side.

"I'm telling you, he's gay," I heard Evyan report to the drama club press corps hanging on her every word. "I don't even know if he knows it himself, but he is."

One of the other kids then chimed in with his two cents, and another with hers. It didn't take long for me to realize who they were talking about. For the next twenty minutes of what felt like a scene ripped directly from a cheesy '90s coming-of-age rom-com (which as it turns out are totally based on real life), I stood there, motionless for fear I'd be heard, staring at myself in the mirror and listening to the sound of my heartbeat underscore my friends as they expounded their uncensored theories on me.

Once their gay press conference had come to a close, the whole crew picked up and made its way back out into the hallway toward the elevators. My friend Kelly, who I adored (not only because she looked like Bernadette Peters, but mostly because of that), was the last out the door, and as she turned to close it behind her, looked up and caught a glimpse of me through the sliding bathroom door. Her face went white. I grabbed her by the arm and pulled her into the bathroom with me, locking the door behind us. She started to explain and apologize frantically, but I cut her off and asked her just to sit with me for a few minutes.

A few minutes quickly became almost an hour. By now, Kelly was sitting in the bathtub in her formal, closing ceremony evening wear. I was standing at the sink with my eyes locked on a travel-sized tube of Colgate toothpaste. The room was silent. We both knew exactly what I was getting ready to say. Kelly knew the minute I asked her to sit with me, and I had known since I was about seven years old. I had already come to terms with it in my own mind, I just hadn't said it out loud yet. And although I'd been performing all week in competition, this was one scene I was not prepared for. But now that I'd heard other people say it, and since we were, after all, at a thespian festival, surrounded by nothing but gay people singing show tunes, I figured—no time like the present.

"I'm gay," I finally let out. They were just two tiny words, but as they passed through my lips, they felt like they weighed about a hundred pounds apiece. I instantly felt so much lighter, I almost levitated. We both cried. I fixed Kelly's makeup before we left for the assembly. She'd never been more grateful to have me. It was mutual.

* * * * *

Not long after returning from Tampa, I landed my very first boyfriend. His name was Frank, and though it turned out we had mutual friends, we technically met in an AOL chat room (I was today years old when I finally decided I was ready to admit that). For those of you too young to remember, on the time line of gay dating tools, AOL chat rooms fell somewhere between Grindr and carving your phone number on a bathroom stall in Grand Central Station. Frank went to a different high school, but like me, he was a big shot in his drama department and also heavily involved in regional theatre. Our first in-person meeting was when I went to see him star in a local production of A *Funny Thing Happened on the Way to the Forum*. (Free dating tip: Never pass up an opportunity to watch a potential suitor run around for two hours in good lighting and above-the-knee tunics.) We were two peas in a pod, and had a blast together. It was so new and exhilarating. Frank had been out for years and had more experience than I had. He was my first . . . well, everything!

My mother was quick to notice this new stray addition to my circle of friends. One night after dinner, she came into my room and sat at the foot of my bed.

"So, you seem to be spending a lot of time with this Frank. . . ."

I was lying down, and, anticipating where this was about to go, rolled onto my side, facing away from her. My nose was pressed into the New York skyline painted on my wall.

"Do you like him?"

I said nothing. I looked up at the little yellow windows painted on the black skyline, wishing they were real so I could jump through one of them.

"You know, there's nothing you can possibly tell me about yourself that I don't already know. I've had gay friends my whole life."

And just like that, there was the word, floating in the ether.

"I love my gay friends," she went on. "I prefer them, even."

I didn't know where all these gay friends she was talking about suddenly came from. I certainly didn't remember ever meeting them. I mean, I'm gay five minutes and suddenly my mother's Liza Minnelli at Studio 54? Anyway, I wasn't about to fact-check. I appreciated what she was going for, and thankful she made it so easy on me. Hell, I didn't even have to say anything. There was no drama on her part, no demonstrations of self-pity, no barrage of questions. That said, it would have been strange for her to respond any other way. I often joke that my mother was *trying* to raise the gayest son possible, but you've read the first few chapters of this book. . . . Am I really joking?

In retrospect, I've occasionally and secretly wished she hadn't made it quite so easy for me. So many gay kids—so many of my own friends—are not as fortunate, and while I feel extremely lucky to have such a loving and understanding mom, I sometimes wonder if a slightly more challenging coming-out experience would have toughened me some-how. But in typical Jewish mother fashion, she was nothing but won-derful, dammit. She even offered to alert the rest of our family so that I wouldn't have to. It was like she immediately became my gay agent (my "gaygent").

• • • • •

Then again, any lack of awkwardness or unpleasantness would be well compensated for by my father. My mother had broken the news to him the next day, and that night we all sat around the kitchen table to dis-cuss hot topics. It quickly became an interrogation, and in textbook-narcissistic a-hole-father fashion, his line of questioning had all to do with him.

"How long have you known?? Why are you just telling me about this now??"

"Gerry, that's not how it works . . . ," my mother tried to explain.

He wasn't interested. He was angry, and took this as nothing but a personal affront.

"So that's who this Frank guy is, huh?" he demanded.

"Yes," I muttered.

For all his shortcomings, my father was reasonably tolerant, es-pecially for a man of sixty-four (sixteen years older than my mother). He was in the entertainment business for much of his life, not terri-bly religious, and not emphatically disapproving of homosexuality in general, at least as far as I knew. For whatever reason, though, he was intensely shocked and appalled by the breaking news of his own son's. He couldn't fathom why this was suddenly "coming at him from left field!" I was about to snarkily suggest he calm down with the pearl-clutching by reminding him of all my childhood ballet recitals and those Ruby Slippers I demanded that one Hanukkah, when he abruptly—and for reasons I'll never know—decided to steer the conversation where no parent should ever dare to go.

"You have to understand, Randy, this is very difficult for me! I don't even know what the hell's going on here! I mean, what the hell are you—a pitcher or a catcher?!"

My mother gasped, audibly.

"Oh my god, Gerry, that's horrible! How could you even say that???"

I was mortified. I slumped over in my chair as though I'd just been punched in the gut, but recovered quickly, jumped to my feet, and darted for the stairs.

"Fuck you, Dad," I said as I ran back up to my room.

It was the first time my father and I had ever discussed sports.

6

Donald Trump Is My Father

How's that for a juicy revelation, huh??? If this chapter title alone doesn't sell some books and finally get me a spot on *The View*, I give up.

Fine, it's not quite that black-and-white (or should I say, "orange-and-bottle-blond"?). The former fake president is not really my biological father. (I would have Mary Trumped the shit out of that solid-golden-toilet opportunity and written a tell-all years ago.) But it's also not entirely fake news or one of those hilarious QAnon conspiracy theories. Let me explain. . . .

By now, you've read a bit about the ominous presence looming in our household throughout my childhood, but I thought it might be of significant interest, perhaps even shocking, considering how many people first came to know me as his on-screen archnemesis, that I was in fact spawned by an absolute Donald Trump clone. (I know . . . it's such a "Luke, I am your father" moment!)

I think it's safe to theorize that Trump unleashed an avalanche of father issues on a lot of the country. For many of us from various wide-ranging generations with patriarchies predating the last third of the twentieth century, when Apple started manufacturing the more modern "good dad" models, he was an avatar for all the worst characteristics possessed by our own shitty dads. More than just unpleasant triggers, for me personally, the similarities have always been downright eerie.

I'm not talking politics. I don't mean my father was a conservative Republican (but then again, neither is the other guy). Like Trump, my father didn't have a strong moral code or belief system about anything, really, aside from his beliefs that he was always right about everything, that he was always the victim in every situation, and that he should always be adored by everyone. (I suppose one could rudely suggest that I inherited some of these beliefs about myself, but I'm *actually* adorable, so I happen to be right about that one. Omg, why are you attacking me?!?!)

My father, Gerry, was born in the Bronx, New York, in 1935, just thirty-five miles from the laboratory in Queens where Trump escaped after being created by evil Russian scientists roughly a decade later. (I *think* that's how it played out.) His mannerisms, down to the cadence of his speaking voice and even some of his facial expressions, made him almost an exact replica of you-know-who. He was a hair-obsessed, lying, cheating, emotionally stunted, and completely self-absorbed textbook narcissist. (And those were his most appealing qualities.) His years as a moderately successful wedding singer and drummer addicted him not only to the glow of the spotlight and cheering crowds, but to his stage makeup. He regularly wore foundation way too dark for his natural complexion, on- and offstage.

In case you're still not sold on the premise of this chapter's heading, he too had a total of three marriages. He met his first wife in his early twenties. We'll call her "Ivana." That marriage produced two daughters (my half sisters). He wound up ditching them for his second wife—I guess we'll refer to her as "Marla"—who had children of her own and who he eventually also left just before meeting my mother around the late 1970s. He was in demand as a musician working for my grandfather (my mom's father), who was the head bandleader at the Huntington Townhouse, a popular catering hall on Long Island. My mom was doing office work for the Townhouse at the time. She and my father began a romantic affair in November of 1979 and married the following March. (No, it was not a shotgun wedding. I, of course, was not born until 1983 . . . 1986 . . . 1998.)

Let's be clear, my mother was and is no Melania. Yes, she was sixteen years younger than my father, and of course, she's smoking hot, but the parallels end there. My mother—a freakishly intelligent, abnormally responsible, highly ethical, and independent working professional—has always been the complete antithesis of the man she married. She was definitely more his fierce rival than First Lady. I guess in this analogy she'd be Hillary Clinton. I don't know who that makes me, but I'll be damned if I'm gonna fuckin' play Ivanka. Ugh, fine . . . I'll be Tiffany.

• • • • •

So why would my mother even pair up with this guy in the first place (other than to produce the cutest baby the world had ever known, of course)? She'll drop by a little later in the book to tell you herself, but I'll try to sum it up for now. For one thing, she was wooed by his charms. Say what I will about my father, he had a certain panache (in a low-rent Dean Martin wannabe sorta way). She was twenty-eight. He was forty-four and a smooth operator—reasonably handsome, with a lovely and respectable crooner's singing voice. It was obvious by his sleazy and embarrassing flirtations with my high school girl friends in later years that he'd been quite the player in his day.

He was also a full-time bullshit artist. The story goes that he originally learned to play the drums as a young boy because the man his mother was having an affair with at the time was a drummer himself. She made my father take lessons from him to cover her own tracks and taught him to lie for her if ever anyone suspected there was something shady going on, which of course there was. It was a lesson he carried with him throughout his entire life. He was a great drummer and an even better liar.

During their courtship, he presented himself to my mother as an innovative entrepreneur and successful businessman. In reality, he was something of a ne'er-do-well and conman (a reputation verified by almost everyone who ever went into business with him). In addition to his music career, he always had side gigs. He was modestly ambitious, but his ambition never really motivated him beyond his half-assed endeavors in multilevel marketing and various get-rich-quick schemes.

It wasn't long before my mother got wise to his games. Shortly after their wedding, a letter came from the IRS. Turned out, my father hadn't paid taxes in almost a decade. (Any of this sound familiar?) It fell to my mother and her father, who hired his own tax attorney to represent his new forty-four-year-old son-in-law, to dig my father out of his mess.

• • • • •

Though he was amenable to starting yet another family when they met, my mother (on the cusp of her thirtieth birthday) was certainly more enthusiastic about the idea. Too young to know anything about his sordid transgressions, I was somewhat indifferent to my father until around age nine. Aside from a few typical temper tantrums, he was pretty good with me during that stage. Though not quite as hands-on as my mother would have liked, he participated and was loving to me. Sometimes he'd take me to work with him. When I was around ages five and six he'd bring me along on his gigs and prop me up behind his microphone onstage to amuse the audience.

It was around the time we moved to Florida that things started getting much worse. He was not doing well professionally or financially. He had just made a bad business deal, which was the reason we left New York in the first place. He was depressed and had a lot of rage, which he took out on my mom and me. We were an unwelcome audience to the man behind the curtain. At home, he couldn't maintain the phony bravado he projected onstage or on phone calls with his precious clients, and he didn't like the idea of his true self being exposed like that—not even to his own family. To him, we were a reflection of the disappointment he felt in himself, and as a result, he resented us.

He eventually found some success again as an entertainment agent in the South Florida condo circuit. During busy seasons when money was coming in, he would be slightly more pleasant at home. Still, his mood swings were exhausting to navigate, which is why I spent most of my time locked in my room. His resentment hit new heights when I hit puberty. I was no longer just a cute accessory for him to show off at gigs or a wide-eyed little kid he could try to impress by acting like a big shot behind the desk at his office. I was growing into an actual person and growing wiser to his tricks and vulnerabilities by the day. He was threatened by that. He now viewed me as an adversary. I also represented the youth and future he no longer had. A lot of the resentment he harbored for me turned to jealousy.

He was extremely verbally and emotionally abusive to us—constant name-calling, door-slamming, and the kind of venomous berating and belittling that would catch you off guard if it came from your worst enemy. Aside from lunging at me a few times, he never actually put his hands on either of us, but the threat of physical violence always seemed imminent. He was so out of control.

One day he came home from work to find me with some of his music equipment set up in the living room after school. I'd taken his microphone, stand, and amplifier out of the garage to get my karaoke on with an impromptu Mariah Carey tribute concert. He walked in on me living my "sweet, sweet fantasy, baby" and to say he threw a fit would be an understatement. It was like that scene in *The Little Mermaid* where King Triton walks in on Ariel getting all horny for a human statue and trashes her grotto, but without the animated pectoral bulges and with much more adult language.

"What the fuck do you think you're doing?" he bellowed.

"I was just singing. I was gonna put it—"

"You got a lot of fuckin' nerve using my things. You put that all back where you found it now. And if you ever touch it again, I'll know."

From then on, all my after-school karaoke concerts were set up to face the front window, so I could rush his equipment back to the garage when I saw his car rounding the cul-de-sac.

Though he was clearly not too generous when it came to donating his own resources for my rehearsal sessions, he was very pleased with my proclivity for performing outside of our living room. To his credit, he came to every dance recital and high school musical I ever did, and always expressed great pride for me in those moments. They were the only times I felt truly seen and respected by him. I think he saw my onstage efforts as an extension of his own talent, and made no bones about staking his claims on my personal achievements.

When I finally started losing some of my baby fat around twelfth grade, friends and family began to compliment my on my transformation. For the first time ever, I was getting positive attention for my physical appearance. I was really proud of all the hard work I'd done on my diet and exercise program. My father took notice and called me into the den for a meeting. He was holding a stack of old pictures which turned out to be of male relatives from his side of the family, and proceeded to give a TED Talk about how exceptional and attractive each one was.

"If anyone ever tells you you're good-looking or talented," he said earnestly, "just remember, I gave that to you. That's my side of the family. You have me to thank."

"Okay . . . ," I said, creeping backward, unable to escape fast enough. "Sure thing! Thanks for the . . . uh . . . awesome DNA! See ya later!"

• • • • •

Ten years after I finally got the hell out of my father's house, he started emailing me regularly. We'd barely spoken since I moved back to New York. His emails were particularly schmaltzy, and he was suddenly determined to "rekindle our relationship" (a notion that made me chuckle to myself as it conjured the image of a bag of dog shit on fire). I had no idea what he was talking about, and frankly neither did he. By now he and my mother were separated and had begun the divorce process, he was living alone, none of his children were speaking to him, and his health was declining. He was alone and he was desperate.

After many nights tossing and turning on the subject, I mustered just enough compassion to give him half a chance—but on my terms. I wrote a lengthy reply telling him I could possibly forgive certain things but only if he acknowledged his abusive behavior through the years and finally accepted some accountability for it. I listed several specific examples of his misdemeanors from my childhood, which I told him had left indelible scars that were impacting me as an adult. I really opened up. I was in my thirties now and he was, as it turned out, nearing the end of his life. "If not now," I figured, "when?"

I also tried to strike a bargain by offering further reconciliation on the condition that he treat my mother fairly in their settlement. I was as temperate and mature in tone as I could be and ended by saying I was hopeful we could move forward, but not until he agreed.

Unsurprisingly, he had no interest in hearing the truth (it was his kryptonite, after all), and no time for my emotions because they didn't flatter him or serve his own agenda. His reply came quickly and in all caps. (Sound familiar?)

RANDY—YOU ARE SO FULL OF SHIT IT'S COMING OUT OF YOUR EARS. MAYBE WHEN YOU GROW UP AND BECOME A MAN YOU'LL REALIZE THE MISTAKE YOU'VE MADE IN NOT CHOOSING TO HAVE A RELATIONSHIP WITH YOUR ONE-AND-ONLY FATHER. I FIND YOU TO BE A SELFISH SON OF A BITCH.

It was a familiar trick of his. He'd extend an affectionate hand every so often, trying to get his own emotional needs met, and the second it became apparent I too was a human with my own needs and emotions, his claws would come out and he'd tear into me. (Trust issues? Party of one?)

He went on victim-playing and lambasting me with profanity-laced non sequiturs, saving his dramatic bombshell for last. He told me I was lucky to have gotten the amount of attention he gave me . . . that his two daughters never got that amount of attention from him . . .

. . . AND YOUR BROTHER HASN'T SEEN OR HEARD FROM ME UNTIL RECENTLY. SURPRISE!!! I HAVE ANOTHER SON! HE'S 40 AND HIS NAME IS GERRY, JR. HE'S A VERY SUCCESSFUL BUSINESSMAN AND I'M SO PROUD OF HIM. I WOULD HAVE TOLD YOU SOONER, BUT YOU'RE SO WRAPPED UP IN YOUR OWN BULLSHIT, YOU NEVER EVEN ASKED ABOUT ME OR MY LIFE.

Surprise, indeed! This was the first time in my life I'd ever heard him refer to another son. I knew by now to take everything he said with a grain of salt. He was famous for his fabrications. But this was too twisted a "big lie" to pull out of thin air, even for him. I brought it to my mother, who filled me in. Apparently, this mystery man was the son of my father's second wife (you know . . . "Marla Maples"). Junior had popped up—unbeknownst to me—a few times throughout the years, claiming to be my father's biological son. My father rejected the claim every time, assuring my mom he only stepfathered him briefly before leaving his ex-wife (Junior's mother). The ex-wife was in a pickle, so my father agreed to sign the birth certificate and let her use his name, but the boy's real father was actually the man my father's ex-wife was with before she met my father. (Is any of this making sense? I have a headache just trying to explain it.)

According to my mom, my father refused to take a paternity test, so, to this day, I'm not sure anyone knows the whole truth. I've never met this alleged, unlikely-but-possible half-maybe-stepbrother of mine. Out of desperation, my father had apparently rekindled their relationship. He had adamantly denied this story for forty years, but realizing he could now use it as a weapon to try and hurt me, he jumped at the opportunity. Not only was this long-lost son of his suddenly my father's precious namesake, he was more successful than I was and my father liked him more than he liked me. (Oh damn, maybe I'm actually Eric Trump in this story. . . . Great, now I'm *really* fuckin' depressed.)

I never really spoke to my father again after that. He passed away in March of 2017, just weeks after the presidential election, at which point his soul entered the body of Donald Jessica Trump, strengthening his evil force and making it possible for him to destroy Earth as planned.

My mom called to give me the news. I wanted so badly to express some kind of emotion about it—any kind. But I dug right down to the bottom of my soul and, at the risk of being totally on-brand by quoting lyrics from A *Chorus Line,* I felt nothing.

• • • • •

I catch a glimpse of my father in my own reflection every once in a while. As the years go by, the anger I feel turns more to sadness. Not sadness for myself, but for him and how the way he lived his life so selfishly, yet so unaware of himself, ultimately led him to such a lonely ending. There have even been times (and don't you dare tell anyone I told you this) that I've felt brief pangs of sorrow and compassion for Trump. I see my father in him. I see the failure and desperation. I also see the inability to blend his foundation, but that's another story.

Anytime I'm blessed with an opportunity to step onstage in front of an audience—a great big, sold-out audience, much bigger than any audience my father ever played to (not that I'm one to dispute crowd sizes)—I think of Gerry. I thank him for teaching me what not to be, for the handful of good qualities I inherited from him (surname included), and for not letting me use his microphone. I suppose it made me work hard enough to get my own. I hope, wherever he is, he's proud of me. I also hope he feels like a real shithead.

From my very personal standpoint, so much of the endless public conversation about Trump has just been echoes of conversations my family and I have been having for decades about our own personal Trump variant. So I'm not at all surprised people have responded strongly to my digs at him, or my perceptions about his character or lack thereof. If I appear insightful on the subject, it's no coincidence. In some ways, I've been talking to my own father the whole time. And if, by any means, I've been an antidote to Donald Trump, perhaps it's because there's always been a little bit of the virus coursing through my veins, helping me fight the infection. I guess you could say I'm fully vaccinated.

7

I'm a Pretty Gurl, Momma

"Ladies and gentlemen, please welcome to the Mermaid Lounge Frank and Randy!"

It was our first night onstage aboard the MS *Regal Empress* cruise ship (and the last goddamn time in history I'd ever accept second billing, believe you me). After miraculously graduating from high school, I spent a lot of time in self-reflection, trying to decide what the hell to do with myself. All my friends had gone on to college, but in the grand tradition of *moi*, I swam against the current and decided to continue living at home for a while, much to my father's dismay. I think because of my theatrical achievements in high school, everyone expected me to take the obvious path, go on to some musical theatre conservatory, and then pound the pavement in New York. I just didn't feel ready. Maybe I simply didn't have the courage.

I eventually tried a semester at Broward College, but when Frank, who was still my boyfriend, called to tell me a friend of his in the industry had offered to hook us both up with jobs on a Caribbean cruise sailing out of Tampa, I told him if he was going, I was going. All we needed were our passports, a ride to Tampa, and, like, forty-two pairs of white pants.

A few weeks later, we were a couple of dames at sea. Our name tags read SOCIAL STAFF & ENTERTAINMENT, which meant that by day we were handcuffed to a packed schedule starting at 6:00 A.M. that included checking out books to guests in the library, calling bingo in the ballroom, and hosting horse racing games by the pool. By night, we got to sing in the Mermaid Lounge as pre-entertainment for a handful of drunken guests before the "real" singers and performers did their shows on the main stage.

Frank and I sang a few solos each before our grand finale, which was an electrifying medley from the musical *Side Show* featuring the two of us as conjoined twin sisters—ya know, just in case the audience hadn't already guessed that we were fucking.

That leads me to the rest of our time aboard the *Empress*, which, thanks to a shortage of crew cabins that allowed us to shack up together in a tiny room on a lower deck, was spent exploring the awkward and occasionally unpleasant joys of gay teen love. (Leo DiCaprio and Kate Winslet we were *not*.) I'll spare you the intimate, if not wildly resourceful, details of our nautical sexcapades, but suffice it to say, it was while floating on the Caribbean Sea that I learned Suave mint-lavender shampoo is only pleasantly invigorating on one's scalp.

• • • • •

After a month of ballroom bingo, Mermaid Lounging, and countless bottles of shampoo, Frank and I both decided we'd had enough. We agreed to give our notice, and then (like the professionals we were) called our mommies and asked them to pick us up as soon as we docked in Tampa a few days later. We spent our final nights on the ship plotting a club act for the two of us. Our plan was to ask my father, who was now working as a talent agent supplying entertainment to the South Florida condo circuit, to book us. It would be the asshole of show business, so to speak—maybe even more so than singing in the Mermaid Lounge— but at least we'd be together.

On the drive home with our moms, something seemed off. It was a gray, rainy day, and the vibe was altogether murky. My mother was especially testy (not just because of the money she'd wasted on all those white pants she bought me), and everyone was being oddly quiet. Even Frank seemed to stop making eye contact with me. After forty-five min- utes or so, we pulled over into a rest stop. While I used the bathroom, my mother cornered Frank inside the convenience store and went full mama bear, telling him he *had* to tell me what his mother had told her on their way to pick us up . . . and he had to tell me now. It turned out, Frank had secretly arranged to go back on the cruise ship the following week, without me.

· · · · ·

A few months later, I was finally over the devastation of my surprise back seat breakup, but still no closer to figuring out what to do with my life. I was also single and ready to mingle. My days were spent working retail at the local mall in stores like Banana Republic and Brookstone, where I'd mostly just sit in the massage chairs and look at boys. After work, I started taking daily walks to the park near our house and run- ning a few laps around the track. It helped clear my mind and lift my spirits.

It was 2001, and gay television was all the rage. My mother and I had standing Thursday-night dates to watch *Will & Grace*, which was in its prime. It was a blissful weekly experience. Not only would we laugh our asses off at what was just undeniable grade A situation comedy, we also delighted in the unspoken comfort of what we both recognized was a mainstream celebration and normalization of, well, me. It was incredibly special on many levels.

Sunday nights were reserved for *Sex and the City* and *Queer as Folk* (the Canadian-American version based on the British series of the same name). To avoid the awkward peril of having to sit together through countless sex scenes, Mom and I enjoyed both of *these* shows from the comfort of our respective bedrooms. As is often the case with art, some depictions and plot lines on QAF may not have stood the test of time, but it was the first show I'd ever seen explore the complexities and relationships of gay men and women. It made me excited to get out there and experience some of my own. It also made me excited to fit into tight outfits.

In addition to my daily track runs, I started watching what I ate and added some Tae Bo and Richard Simmons's *Sweatin' to the Oldies* workout tapes I'd found in a spare room closet to my weekly regimen. Before long, friends and family were complimenting me on my noticeable weight loss. One day while driving to work, I stopped at a red light and looked up at myself in the rearview mirror to find something strange.

"What the hell is that?" I asked myself. They were . . . cheekbones! And lips! Holy shit, I almost had a face! My baby fat had finally started melting away, and for the first time in a long time, I didn't hate the reflection staring back at me. Hell, it was kinda cute! On my next visit to the eye doctor, I was fitted for my first pair of contact lenses, and before I knew it, my growing list of discernible facial features even included a pair of eyes.

It was no coincidence that I began to notice other changes, too. I was getting more attention—a new kind—and not just from friends and family. Suddenly, some of the boys I was looking at in the mall started looking back. Some of them would actually come into the store where I was working to talk to me or give me their phone numbers. It was just like *Sex and the City*! Unfortunately, I was still living with my parents, and it was still the wrong city.

● ● ● ● ●

I had a new look and a new attitude. I even started wearing solid T-shirts (so long, Tasmanian Devil!). It was a strikingly impressive transformation, if I do say so myself, the likes of which had not been seen since Olivia Newton-John emerged as "bad Sandy" at the end of *Grease*. I started auditioning again, and was soon working steadily in children's theatre productions in Miami, entertaining schoolkids on weekdays.

I was cast as "the bellhop" in the White-Willis Theatre's production of the play *Lend Me a Tenor*. It was a small featured role, but it was the comic relief and I relished every second of it. I don't know if it was the weight loss or the bit of maturity that came with whatever life experience I now had under my belt, but I felt myself pushing through to new places onstage, and allowing myself the freedom to really be funny in a way I'd never been in front of an audience before. Local newspapers came to review us and all highlighted me as the show's breakout star. A few of them compared me to one of my comedy idols, Jerry Lewis, which thrilled me. I felt the best I ever had in my own skin, and was getting positive reinforcement all over the place!

"This is nice," I thought. "Whatever it is, let's have more!"

Having more meant eating less. I kicked my diet and exercise routine into overdrive. I was now subsisting on a few hundred calories per day, and checking the scale compulsively. I'd allow myself ten grapes for breakfast and another ten for lunch. If I splurged on more than that, it meant skipping dinner, or adding a few laps around the track to make up for it. After a run in the hot Florida sun one afternoon, I got back to the house and went up to my bathroom to wash up. The room started spinning, my legs started wobbling out from under me, and I fell to the floor. I blacked out for a few seconds before coming to. I was scared as hell and so malnourished.

My friend Sami, who was doing children's theatre with me, was the first to intervene on one of our morning carpools to Miami.

"You look like shit. Everyone in the show is asking me if you're sick. You need to gain some weight."

I didn't like hearing that people were talking, but had no intention of taking her advice. I couldn't stop what I was doing. I didn't know how.

There was concern among family members, too, but other than Nanny trying to tempt me with bread and ice cream any chance she got, not much was done about it. My mother would make passing remarks about seeing my bones sticking through my T-shirts, but she had a long history of her own food issues, and at the time, I don't think she really know how to handle mine.

· · · · ·

After *Lend Me a Tenor* closed, I landed a role in a regional production of *South Pacific*. The director liked how I sang "Younger Than Springtime" in the audition and cast me as Lieutenant Joe Cable, the strapping young U.S. Marine and love interest of Liat, a beautiful young Polynesian girl living on the island. I think once rehearsals began, though, he quickly realized I was more of a Nellie Forbush (accent on the "nellie").

"Make him stronger, Randy!" the director shouted from the back of the theatre as we bumbled through our big love scene. "She needs to fall in love with him! Butch it up!"

I was sweating bullets all over the poor girl playing Liat, and too hungry to focus. I was butching it up the best I could, but it kept coming out less John Kerr and more Mitzi Gaynor. I needed a cosmo and a sandwich.

A few days later, I walked into the theatre for rehearsal, and to my surprise, saw one of the chorus boys onstage, doing *my* blocking and singing *my* song. What the hell kind of *42nd Street*, "Lullaby of Broadway," bullshit was this???

He sounded lousy but looked terrific—butch as they come. The assistant director caught me standing like a statue in the back of the house, and ran to greet me as she pushed me back out into the lobby.

"What's going on?" I asked her.

"We're just trying something out. We love how the songs sound on you, but we're just thinking we might want to go in a different direction."

It seemed their problem wasn't "Younger Than Springtime," but that I was—as the song goes—"gayer than laughter."

"Maybe you two will alternate? We haven't figured it out yet. . . ."

She kept talking as I walked out the front door, never to return to *South Pacific* again. (Bali-bye, gurl!) Who needed it anyway? It was just some third-rate production . . . but it now had me second-guessing my whole damn life! What was I doing anyway? What was the goal? Was this the career I wanted? And even if it was, did it want me back? Ugh, I was having a Pippin moment. Where did I belong???

My singing voice was all over the map and didn't fall neatly into any of the boxes they make you tick on audition forms. I didn't have a firm grasp on what type I was or how the hell to market myself. Sure, I was a passable Sky Masterson in high school (literally . . . I passed science class because of it), but knew I'd be considered too "queeny" to play the straight male ingénues out in the real world. At the same time, I didn't feel big or broad enough to play the comedic sidekicks. And how many bellhops could I play? If I moved to New York, would I keep getting pushed backed out into the lobby? And all that aside, without formal training or a college degree, who would want me anyway?

Suddenly, I was very unclear about what lay ahead, and which career path I should take. Maybe I'd have to find another one. Maybe none of the paths I had to choose from would ever be right for me. Maybe I'd have to carve my own.

8

Chicken

I had just turned twenty-one in the summer of 2002 (and if you dare stop to do the math I'll kill you). The Florida heat felt more oppressive than ever, but it had little to do with climate change. The cocoon I had spun myself into post high school, post cruise ship, was really beginning to suffocate me. I was ready to spread my wings and leave my parents' nest but had no idea in which direction to fly . . . or if I even knew how to fly.

Most of my friends had left the state. My eating disorder was still raging. My lack of control over my life led to a greater need for the false sense of control I got from dieting. Dinners were now limited to a few pieces of dried fruit from snack bags I'd spend hours selecting from drugstore shelves, obsessing exhaustively over caloric content. The children's theatre productions were keeping me somewhat busy and minimally creative, but paid shit. The supplemental temp work I started taking, mostly doing data entry in poorly lit office buildings, was a living hell, and the pressure from my parents to find something more stable was growing by the minute.

My mother was up in my room one night, sitting in her usual spot at the foot of my bed, giving one of her lectures to the back of my head.

"You're gonna have to figure something out soon. You have to start making some decisions. . . . What are you gonna do?"

The phone on my nightstand rang. I picked it up, motioning for Mom to leave and close the door behind her. It was my friend Sami. She was still carpooling with me almost every day to Miami for children's theatre, so I'd been spending a lot of time with her and her boyfriend Mickey. They were all I had left. I could tell she was itching to tell me something right away.

"We're moving to New York," she said in a tizzy, before I could ask what was up.

Sami, who I'd first met as a kid at the Hollywood Playhouse (we dated seriously for about three days back then), was a few years older than I was, and on the cusp of a quarter-life crisis of her own. She and Mickey knew they wanted to get the hell out of South Florida, and they decided the time was now. They were both extremely talented musicians, but had no real plan, and that suddenly sounded like a great plan to me.

As Sami ran through their moving agenda, I looked around at the mural of Manhattan surrounding me—the black paint now chipping in some spots. All those fake, two-dimensional buildings on my bedroom wall suddenly looked faker and more flat than ever. I started to hate them. I think I'd been outgrowing my fantasy for a while. Maybe this was the kick in the ass I needed to push me into reality.

I told Sami I was happy for her, and hung up without making any mention of my own plans. I still didn't *have* any of my own plans by the time the phone hit the receiver, or for the ten minutes following, as I sat there in silence. Eventually, Mom knocked on my door.

"Who was that?"

"It was Sami," I told her. "She and Mickey are moving to New York City. . . . I'm gonna go, too." I don't know why I said it. I don't even think I'd really thought it to myself before I did. It just fell out.

As much as I was yearning to "mingle with the old-time throng" on Broadway, I was in no way equipped for big-city living. I was an overly sheltered mama's boy, scared of my own shadow. 9/11 had only happened a little less than a year earlier. I barely knew how to do my own laundry and have always had an awful sense of direction—even in utero. I was a cesarean birth because as a fetus, I was apparently trying to go *up* the birth canal instead of come down! Trying to figure out the New York subway system gave me panic attacks, even during our brief summer vacations. I had no place to live, no job prospects, and less than two hundred dollars in my bank account. What in the fuck was I thinking?

• • • • •

The rap on me, as retold by my mother countless times, is that I never crawled as a baby. One day, I just got up and walked across the room. From then on, I walked everywhere, without ever falling down. I took a little longer than most of the other babies, but when I was ready, I just walked.

"Okay," Mom said without blinking an eye. She'd have lots of questions and concerns about my decision later on, but in that moment, I think she realized that I was ready to start walking.

• • • • •

Less than a month later, my uncle Andrew was picking me up at the airport on Long Island. I was right back where I started, but this time, I was on my own. On the drive to his house, Andrew asked, "So . . . what are you gonna do?"

There was that goddamn question again! I didn't know what I was gonna do! Why did people keep asking me that? I was skinny, dammit! Wasn't that enough?!?

My short-term plan was to stay with Andrew for a week until it was time to meet my old childhood chum Courtney at her great-aunt's vacant apartment in Manhattan. Courtney (who had since forgiven me for stealing the role of Snow White from her in my backyard some thirteen years prior) was still living on Long Island but staying in the city for a few weeks to grind through her final callbacks for the Broadway production of *Mamma Mia!* She agreed to let me stay with her. While Courtney was busy "Voulez-Vousing" during the day, I was schlepping around midtown with a stack of résumés, asking every manager in every retail shop and restaurant I came upon to take a chance on me, and gimme, gimme, gimme, some money, money, money. (And if you didn't get that last round of ABBA references, you can leave right now.)

A week had passed, and not one of my job applications had led to a single return phone call. I guess that's the name of the game (sorry—that is my last ABBA reference for this chapter, I swear). This had clearly been a big mistake. What was I doing? My friend was getting callbacks to serve jump splits in Broadway shows and I couldn't even get one to serve limp breadsticks at the Olive Garden?! What the actual fuck?? I was just about ready to hightail it back to Florida when Courtney had a perfect, awful idea. She'd picked up a few summer shifts at the Hooters restaurant on Broadway and Fifty-Sixth Street for extra cash, and wanted me to go in with her that afternoon to apply for a job.

"You're a few pounds late on that one, sweetie," I joked. My chest was the flattest it had ever been.

"I'm serious," she said. "The general manager is gay. He'll fucking love you."

Sure enough, he fucking did. We hit it off instantly, sitting there at an overly lacquered wooden cocktail table, surrounded by infinite bottles of hot sauce and the musk of sweaty chicken wings. I made him laugh, batted my eyelashes a few times, and before I knew it, I was the first male host in history ever to grace the entryway of Hooters NYC. (Fine, I'm not completely sure that little factoid is historically accurate. But it must be, right??? Anyway, I'm the hero in this book, so we're going with it.) It wasn't exactly the career move I had in mind, but it was a job. And hey! I was—technically speaking—on Broadway.

I know what you're thinking/hoping, but no, I did not get to wear the tiny orange nylon shorts. I was confined to a pair of boring khakis and a white polo shirt. Sorry to disappoint you! But if you think *you're* disappointed, imagine all those poor, horny construction workers and businessmen who would walk through the front door on their lunch breaks or after work for some beer and boobs to find Randy Rainbow standing there with his pink clipboard! ("Hey, gurl!") I must have single-handedly depressed more Wall Street stockbrokers than the Crash of 1929.

· · · · ·

My job problem was solved for the moment, but my time on Courtney's aunt's pullout was about to expire. I spent the next few months surfing the sofas of family friends and long-lost relatives who lived in the area. Finally, one of the gals from Hooters asked if I'd be interested in rooming together. Now with a steady income and a little money saved, I jumped at the chance. We quickly found a freshly renovated basement apartment in Astoria, Queens—a charming and newly trendy neighborhood that would become my beloved home for the next seventeen years, and the place where my life would really begin.

One Saturday afternoon, I was checking out the area around our apartment. While walking down Steinway Street, I passed a pet shop with a litter of tiny, tan Persian kittens in the window. They were obscenely doll-faced and adorable. Noticing my googly eyes through the glass (and hoping to make a sale), the shop owner invited me in for a closer look.

"Go in back. I meet you there," he directed me.

Before I could tell him I had no money to spend, I was ushered into a small room where he and his assistant proceeded to unleash the entire litter of kittens at my feet (sneaky bastards). They all instantly fled to a corner and huddled together in terror—all but one. One little guy stood determined and fearless in the middle of the room. He leaned back on his hind legs, put both front paws on my shoe, and locked his big brown eyes with mine.

"What the hell kind of Disney movie trickery is this?" I thought. It was love at first sight, for both of us, but I had to force myself out of the room.

"I'm sorry," I told the owner as I ran back out to Steinway Street. "I don't have the money."

• • • • •

Okay, okay . . . Before I go on, I want to acknowledge the fact that some of you are likely triggered by the notion that I would even consider buying a kitten from a store. Trust me, I hear you. I grew up with dozens of cats in our home ever since I was a baby, and they were all adopted from shelters. But what can I say? This is how it happened, and I want to be honest with you. Besides, this little guy deserved love, just like the rest of us.

• • • • •

A few days later, I was down in Florida, visiting my family. Mom and Nanny asked me about my friends, my job, my new apartment . . . but all I could talk about was this amazing kitten I'd just met. My father took note and before I got on the plane back to New York a few days later, he handed me an envelope with cash in it. He told me if the cat was still at the pet shop when I got home, I should get him. He knew what a challenge it was for me to be out on my own, and I think this was his way of showing support. It remains my fondest memory of my father, and the thing for which I'll always be most grateful to him.

Courtney went back to the pet shop with me the following week. As fate would have it, there was my buddy, still in the window. Courtney suggested I name him Mushi because—well—he was mushy. Sold!

* * * * *

Back at work, I was quickly becoming the most popular Hooters girl in town. As you can imagine, the jovial gay boy at the host stand was a refreshing sanctuary for the waitresses and bartenders getting hit on by greasy horndogs all day. Before long, I was their official mascot. It was a job I did not take lightly, and one that would soon involve an unexpected responsibility: Celebrity Public Relations.

The girls started inviting me to join them and their hot-as-fuck boyfriends on after-work social outings. One night, after a few too many mango margaritas at our usual downtown hot spot, one of the girls pulled me outside and pushed me into the back of a stretch limousine parked in front of the building.

"I'm gonna go get the others," she said, slamming the limo door and leaving me alone with a giant man seated next to me.

"Oh, hello," I slurred, noticing him suddenly.

"Hey, how ya doin'?" he politely responded, not sure what to make of me.

"Wouldn't *you* like to know," I flirted back. He laughed . . . hard.

During the awkward silence that followed, I got a call on my cell. It was my mother, just checking in before bed.

"Where are you?" she asked.

"I'm in the back of a limo with this guy," I said, trying to hide my drunken drawl.

"What??? What guy?"

"This guy! He . . . hey . . . what's your name?"

He told me his name and though it meant nothing to me, when I repeated it to my mother, she shrieked. It turned out he was a very high-profile, mega, major-league all-star athlete (still meant nothing to me). My mother brought me up to speed and I hung up, playing it cool. I was just about to ask him if he was a pitcher or a catcher when the limo door opened. The rest of my crew piled in and we headed to another club.

Now, I'm not saying this man—who we'll just call "Joe Baseball" for now—was or was not married at the time, nor am I speculating that he may or may not have been having an extramarital fling with one of my waitress companions. I'm just saying it's amazing what shenanigans went on before the days of social media. I can't imagine he would have been quite so conspicuous just a few years later. (PS: If you ever run into me at a party and buy me a couple of mango margaritas, I might spill the beans.)

For the next several months, we spent a lot of time with Joe Baseball—on planes, in Jacuzzis, at backyard barbecues . . . He let me try on his World Series ring one day. It fit me like a bracelet. He'd fly us around to wherever he was spring training, put us up in penthouse suites, and even surprise us with shopping sprees from time to time—all expenses paid. It was good to be a Hooters girl! (I still had no idea who he was.)

• • • • •

My lady friends weren't the only ones turning heads at the restaurant. A new regular started coming in every day for lunch. On his way out, he'd stop at the podium to talk to me. He was in his forties, tall, and fairly handsome, with salt-and-pepper hair. No all-star athlete, but hey, it was slim pickings for a Hooters boy. Anyway, I had no reason to think he was flirting, or even gay for that matter. (Do Manhattan gays eat chicken wings?)

One afternoon, he got a little more personal and asked what I did when I wasn't "manning the chicken coop." I told him I was an actor.

"Are you in anything now?"

"No, not right now. I just moved here not too long ago. Trying to save some money."

As he handed me his card, he told me his name was Alan and that he was a comedy producer.

"I'm actually looking for an assistant. If you wanna pick up a few extra bucks and some experience, give me a call."

It seemed like a great opportunity. I'd always been interested in comedy, of course, but never professionally considered it—certainly not from a production angle. And while the glamorous perks of my Hooters lifestyle had their occasional appeal, the job was not fulfilling. I was finally in New York City—the Promised Land! I could see the lights of Broadway just down the street, but aside from my infrequent splurges on half-priced tickets at the TKTS booth to see *Thoroughly Modern Millie* or *Aida*, my dreams still felt as far away as they ever had. I was still so afraid, but also itching to at least dip my toe in show business.

A week later, I was reporting to Alan's office for what we decided would begin as a part-time trial. While he was in fact a legitimate producer, affiliated with some well-known comedy brands and multiple film, television, and radio projects, his tiny midtown office was no major operation. Aside from answering a few phone calls, there was not much for me to do. I spent most mornings sitting and watching him respond to emails until it was time for lunch. He insisted on taking me to the Planet Hollywood in Times Square every day because he had a strange obsession with their Cap'n Crunch chicken strips. Hoping to gain some industry insight, I'd try to ask him questions about his business, but he'd ultimately find a way to turn the conversation back on me. He'd interview me about my childhood, my interests, my aspirations . . . I told him I was still figuring it all out.

"You're pretty . . . ," he said.

Well, that stopped me in my tracks. He went on.

"If you keep yourself thin for the next few years, you can do anything you want." I thought, "Gee . . . thanks?" I suppose this odd little motivational speech was meant to bolster my confidence, but what it actually did was gross me out and make my palms sweaty while simultaneously exacerbating the anxiety I was feeling as I forced myself to resist the stunningly crunchy, yet highest-calorie chicken strips known to humankind.

After about a week, his lunchtime interviews started getting progressively more intimate. Questions about what I was interested in professionally soon became questions about what I was into sexually. I tried to laugh them off, but it was agonizing. The more I'd deflect, the more he'd persist. I was still so young—even younger than my age. I didn't realize I could have just told him to stick his chicken strips where the sun didn't shine. It didn't occur to me to just get up and leave. All I kept thinking of were the framed movie posters on the wall in his office. Posters of movies I had actually seen . . . in movie theaters! Posters with his name on them. This was a chance to be part of something real, and to stay in New York. I was being given an opportunity and if it meant sitting through a few creepy lunches, I'd have to bite the bullet.

He was also opening up more about himself. He'd had a kidney transplant years earlier and was still managing some pretty serious health issues.

"I'm not getting any younger," he'd say. "I need someone to take care of me."

These passive-aggressive allusions to his own desire for companionship started coming more and more frequently, and finally turned into blatant solicitations. After a while, there was just no way left for me to respond but with the cold, hard truth.

"Alan, I'm really grateful for the chance to work with you, but if you're looking for a—"

"Hey, I have a meeting with the CEO of a major Broadway website tomorrow." He cut me off before I could say what he didn't want to hear. "I'm gonna see if she'll make you their editor."

These empty promises about professional opportunities became routine. As young as I was, I was still smart enough to realize that this was all a sloppy manipulation game. I'd let it play out, but in no way would I ever fall for it.

* * * * *

It was 11:30 P.M. I had just finished a night shift at Hooters when I got a call from Alan. He was frantic.

"I just fell. I don't know what's wrong. I'm scared. You need to come over."

"What happened? Do you need me to call 911?"

"No, just please come over right away. The door's unlocked."

He hung up and I headed to the nearest subway station. The trains were slow, as usual, and he lived in Brooklyn. By the time I got to his apartment, it was almost 12:45. I knocked and let myself in. The shower was running in the bathroom to my right, and I heard his voice coming from the same place.

"Hey!" He already sounded much calmer than he had on the phone. I walked toward the bathroom and saw him standing naked in the shower.

"What's up, little Randy?" He was clearly not in distress.

"What happened?" I asked, quickly turning away.

"I don't know, it was crazy. I fell in the kitchen. Thought it was kidney stuff. I think I'm okay. You want a drink?"

Exhausted and aggravated, I staggered into his living room. He came out in his bathrobe after a few minutes, still dripping, and perched himself on the arm of the chair where I was sitting.

"Hey, I spoke to that website woman. She wants to set up a meeting with you!"

It was as if nothing had happened. I hopped out of the chair and walked toward the front door.

"Alan, I'm so tired. If you're all good, I'm gonna head home."

"You can stay here if you want. It'll be a nightmare getting a train at this hour."

"Uh . . . ya think?"

After I rejected his sleepover invitation for a sixth time, he finally gave me money for a cab. I glared out the window at New York on the drive home, wondering why the place I loved so much would play me like this. I swore I'd never fall for any of Alan's bullshit again.

· · · · ·

I didn't know if I had just gotten used to him or if he finally started taking the hint, but for the next month, Alan stayed pretty well behaved. He had actually followed through with setting up a few introductory business meetings for me, and was taking me to launch parties and opening-night events where he'd introduce me to big shots.

Late that October, he asked me to take a drive with him to Connecticut for an overnight business trip. One of his friends and colleagues, a well-known film critic, had to record a few voice-overs for an upcoming radio special Alan was producing, and wanted us to do it at his home.

"It'll be good practice for you," Alan said. "Plus the house is gorgeous and you'll get a couple of free meals."

It was dark out when we finally arrived at the house in Connecticut a few nights later. Traffic had been hell. As Alan took his bag out of the back seat, I noticed he was leaving the recording equipment.

"You want me to grab it?"

"No, you can leave it for now."

I followed him up the stone walkway to the front door, which he unlocked with his own key. All the lights were out inside.

"Where's your friend?" I asked.

"Oh, he called when you were in the bathroom at the rest stop. He's stuck in the city. He's not gonna make it."

With that, he flipped a switch and suddenly all of the light bulbs turned on, including the one inside my brain. Was he fucking kidding me?!

"You want something to eat?" he asked, now playing the happy homemaker. I couldn't get away from him quickly enough.

"No, I'm tired. I'm just gonna go to bed. Which room am I in?"

"I don't think he wants us to spread out too much. He has guests coming this weekend and I think he wants to keep the place intact. He's weird about that stuff. We can share his room."

"No, Alan," I said starkly. "I'll just sleep on the couch." I was so over this.

"No, don't do that," he said, defeated. "You can use the guest room. I'll tell him I said it was okay."

I lay there in the dark, staring at the ceiling in the guest room, cursing Alan for pulling this ridiculous stunt, and cursing myself for falling for it. I drifted off while thinking up the speech I would deliver to him the next morning, telling him I wasn't gonna put up with this crap anymore and demanding that he start taking me more seriously. About an hour later, I woke up to Alan's hot breath on the back of my neck. He was in bed with me. His enormous body, which was three times the size of mine, was locked around me in a tight bear hug. He was grinding into me and sloppily kissing my face.

"Alan, stop!" I yelled, still half asleep. I felt like I was being smothered and couldn't catch my breath. He wouldn't let go and he wasn't verbally responding (which was the scariest part). He took his underwear off with one hand, holding me in place with his other arm. I was squirming around like a fish, trying to get out of his grip and pleading with him to get off as he tried forcing himself into me for what felt like five minutes. Finally, he gave up and let go. I ran into the bathroom and locked the door behind me.

"What the fuck is wrong with you?" I heard him say in a muffled voice on the other side. "Jesus, did something happen to you as a kid or something?" (As if the only possible explanation for my rejecting his disgusting advances had to be some unresolved childhood trauma.) I didn't answer. I stayed locked in the bathroom for the rest of the night and eventually fell asleep in the bathtub.

We didn't say one word to each other on the drive home the next morning. It was Halloween—my favorite holiday. The Connecticut scenery was picture-perfect, and all the ritzy houses were decorated to the nines, but I refused to enjoy any of it. I didn't want to retain any pleasant memories—not a single leaf or pumpkin—for fear they would forever be associated with this cockamamie "business trip." Alan dropped me off in Astoria. It was the last time I'd ever see him.

● ● ● ● ●

That night was the Hooters Halloween party. I went as Mary-Kate Olsen and my friend Debbie went as Ashley Olsen (one of us lost a coin toss, but I'll let you guess which one). I told my girlfriends about what had happened the night before. As you can probably imagine, my experience was not unfamiliar to them. One of the girls, Mandy (who fancied herself something of a clairvoyant), told me her friend was a bartender at a popular restaurant down in Chelsea called Cafeteria, and that they were hiring.

"It's definitely more your vibe," she told me. "I think you would be amazing there!"

The next afternoon, I put on my cutest ensemble from Zara and strolled down to apply at Cafeteria. After a couple of interviews, an evening gown competition, and a full glam makeover, they gave me the job! I gave notice at Hooters, tossed my hideous khakis and white polo, and kissed my girls goodbye. A few days later, I was a full-fledged host at one of the swankiest hot spots in Chelsea. Sure, I was still stuck behind a podium taking fried chicken to-go orders, but this time I was in the center of Gay Mecca, surrounded by my people. I was finally a real gay! I was seating supermodels, porn stars, and celebrities the likes of Tyra Banks, Alanis Morissette, Molly Shannon, Idina Menzel, and the original cast of *Queer Eye*! This time, the fried chicken orders I was taking were being picked up by well-dressed bodyguards who then brought them out to the corner of Seventeenth Street and Seventh Avenue for Mariah Carey to devour in the back seat of her limo.

I had finally made it in show business.

9

The Prick in the Balloon

One of my favorite shows as a kid was *Mr. Wizard's World*. For those of you pretending you're too cool or too young to remember, Mr. Wizard was the host of a 1980s Nickelodeon children's program (a revival of the original *Watch Mr. Wizard* from the 1950s) who taught us how to do completely useless parlor tricks using household items, and then blew our freaking minds by explaining the science behind them.

One of the demonstrations that has always stuck with me involved an average red balloon, some Scotch Tape, and a box of corsage pins. Mr. Wizard blew up the balloon, decorated it randomly with six pieces of tape, and then instructed his young kid helper of the day—whose name I believe was Jackie—to stick the pins through each piece of tape on the balloon. I know what you're thinking: "No, Jackie! Don't do it, you foolish girl!" Well, calm down. As Mr. Wizard explains, the Scotch Tape prevents the latex from stretching. Therefore, when the pin passes through the added layer of tape and into the balloon, there's no pop! (I actually still don't understand it myself.) Anyway, Jackie could not have cared less, but my mind was freaking blown.

I've been thinking a lot about that little domestic science experiment while writing this book. Not only 'cause it's just awesome as shit, but because it also perfectly symbolizes my comedy approach. Grab a martini, I'll pretend I'm Mr. Wizard and try to explain:

The pin in the balloon is a cliché comedy metaphor (the balloon representing the setup or tension, and the pin representing the punch line releasing the tension). You never hear about the Scotch Tape, though, which I think is the key ingredient. Without it, you can still get the job done, of course. You can raw-dog that balloon with your little corsage pin all day and it'll pop every time, making a loud noise. Some people will find it shocking or offensive. Some will laugh nervously or simply because they're twelve years old and find humor in the breaking of things. Some will delight in the surprise and relief that instantly follows. And some will just run out of the room.

By adding a layer of tape, you can effectively prick the balloon without making a loud noise. Fewer people will be so quick to run away. In fact, they might be so interested in your little magic trick, they'll come in for a closer look. They might even be happy to learn something! (Unless they're Jackie. Jackie does not care.)

In the balloon/pin comedy metaphor of it all, Mr. Wizard's piece of tape represents the extra layer that makes the comedy special and less "in your face," setting it apart from your run-of-the-mill, setup/punch-line dad jokes. For me, the Scotch Tape is the satire. It's just a small, thin, almost translucent accessory—some people won't even be able to see it, but it makes the whole demonstration more interesting. With a little Scotch tape, you can use the sharpest pins on the largest balloons without an offensive pop. The balloon won't feel a thing, and you might even amuse a few people in the process (except Jackie, of course).

I've never been a fan of loud noises, so this slant on balloon-pricking always appealed to me. In terms of comedy, it would later serve me well when I'd ultimately decide to aim my pins at some pretty big balloons. But I'm getting ahead of myself!

• • • • •

Humor has always been a big part of my life. Even as a kid, I was always interested in the math and science of it (ironically, I had zero interest in math or science in school—go figure). I'd study the comedy performances I loved, trying to figure out exactly what it was about them that moved people to laughter . . . why one of Bea Arthur's pauses on *The Golden Girls* lasted as long or as short as it did, or why one tiny "so" or "and" could make or break an entire line reading on *SNL*.

Sometimes I didn't have to look any further than my own backyard. There are many funny people in my family, mainly on my mother's side. None of them are comedians by trade, but they could have been. My mom, Gwen, and my uncle Andrew are both droll, sardonic Richard Lewis types, and my uncle Josh is basically Jewish Tony Danza, but funnier. It seemed clear to me growing up that New York plus Jewish equaled funny. Having been moved from New York to South Florida at a young age and spending many of my formative years there, I had a unique perspective on my own New York, Jewish family. At family functions, I often felt like an outsider looking in—an audience member. It was like I was a slightly different species. Not like I was a penguin and they were all giraffes or anything. It was more like they were all zebras and I was one of those zebra/donkey hybrids. (A zonkey? A deebra?) I would quietly spectate the tennis match of one-liners and repartee being bounced back and forth across the Thanksgiving dinner table, wondering if I could do that, too.

"These people are fuckin' hilarious," I'd think to myself. "Why don't any of them have agents?"

I also learned early on that humor was more than an amusing sport or parlor trick. It was an essential tool. It was a gift and a superpower, which, if used correctly, could alter perceptions, close divides, and make the most distressing or uncomfortable situations manageable— enjoyable, even!

• • • • •

The day after I told my mother I was gay (or, rather, the day after she told me), I was in the car with Nanny and her friend Suzie. We were on our way to the Broward Mall for some afternoon window-shopping. Nanny was driving and Suzie—a staunch Republican—was up in the passenger's seat. I was in the back, lost in my own thoughts. I knew Mom had probably spoken to Nanny by now, but didn't know if she had broken the news to her or not. I was sweating bullets and too tense to speak. Nanny hadn't said anything about it to me yet, and I had no idea how she would react or when she might bring it up . . . if she ever did.

She and Suzie were in the middle of a heated political debate (standard fare whenever those two got together). Between my impending gay panic attack in the back seat and the rowdy episode of *The View* going on between Nanny and Suzie up front, there was so much tension built up in that car, you could've sliced it with a stiletto. They were both yelling and their argument had just about reached its apex when the yelling finally turned to awkward silence. We stopped at a light, and noticing the zoned look on my face through her rearview mirror, Nanny seized the moment and segued unexpectedly.

"Earth to Randy!"

I straightened up and looked back at her reflection.

"Listen, your mother told me what you told her . . . you know . . . about what you are."

My stomach fell out of my butt. What the fuck . . . wait . . . this was happening right now??? I froze.

"Suzie already knows . . . it's fine."

Apparently Suzie, a close family friend, had been filled in on the drive to pick me up, but I could tell she was just as uncomfortable as I was. Nanny kept right on.

"I just wanna tell you, it doesn't matter to me what you are. I love you and I will always love you, no matter what . . ."

(Pause, two, three . . .)

". . . just as long as you don't wanna be a Republican. They're fuckin' lunatics."

It was the driest, most perfectly timed delivery. Suzie burst into a fit of laughter and then so did I. Suddenly, all my angst was lifted and the fight with Suzie had come to a cease-fire. Nanny had done a magic trick . . . and it was a twofer! With one little pin, she let the air out of two big balloons! A signal went off in her brain alerting her that we were all in need of some respite—a minivacation from that particular moment in time—so she used her superpower to convert all that negative tension into humor and ultimately saved the day.

Of course, the whole thing could have backfired. I could have become even more embarrassed and started crying. Suzie could have been totally offended, stormed out of the car, and incited a violent insurrection at the U.S. Capitol. But Nanny knew she was in a controlled environment. She was a skilled maestro who knew her audience. *Of course* she wasn't *actually* that blasé about her acceptance of me. She wasn't trivializing my coming out. Nor did she *actually* believe her dear friend Suzie was a fucking lunatic (at least not a *complete* fucking lunatic). Suzie and I understood her intention, and that made all the difference. Still, it was a gamble. Popping balloons can be a dangerous practice. There's always a chance that someone could get hurt. But when it works out, that sublime release is the best gift anyone can give or receive.

This was one of many similar episodes that ultimately made me want to use any bit of that superpower I may have been lucky enough to inherit to its fullest potential. I wanted to honor it, and try to hone it so I could spend the rest of my life orchestrating little moments of respite for other people like the one Nanny orchestrated for me in her car that day. What a wonderful and invaluable contribution! Of course it wouldn't be until many years later that I'd even consider it a vocational pursuit, and even longer until I'd get to call it my job.

· · · · ·

As you may have noticed by now, our family was not afraid of a little colorful language from time to time. Language in general was something to be respected—celebrated, even—but never feared. I was thirteen years old when Alanis Morissette's *Jagged Little Pill* album came out (again . . . put down your calculators, assholes!). I was a massive fan and so was my mom. We'd rock out to the CD in her car every day, but it always got more than a little uncomfortable when the time came for lyrics like, *"and are you thinking of me when you fuck her?"* Mom finally decided to pop that balloon one day.

"I think it's so silly how much attention people give to words. They're just words! If we all walked around saying them all the time, they wouldn't be so shocking and then we could just get on with our lives!"

She went on to demonstrate.

"Fuck! Fuck, fuck, fuck, fuck, fuck, fuck! Okay???"

I don't think my mother's fuck-filled sermon on free speech to the tune of "You Oughta Know" was advocating a movement toward desensitizing people to bad words so that we could then go around offending each other all day. I think the philosophy was that by removing the stigma—taking the poison out of words—we could make them less toxic, thereby liberating people from the burden of having to be offended constantly. We've never given much power to offensive words in our family, especially when used artistically. Perhaps it's an inherent defense mechanism that has something to do with our long ancestral history of religious persecution and traditionally being the targets of hate speech. Or perhaps we are just douchebags. Either way, it always made perfectly practical sense to me.

• • • • •

It also makes perfect sense, considering my upbringing and family influence, that I was always most attracted to certain styles of comedy and comedians who weren't afraid to push the envelope, experiment with all the colorful flourishes of language, or turn uncomfortable situations and topics on their ear.

My earliest sparks of interest in comedy on-screen came from shows like *Pee-wee's Playhouse* and the stellar comedic performances of actors like Billy Crystal, Malcolm McDowell, Fred Willard, and Robin Williams in Shelley Duvall's 1980s fairytale anthology, *Faerie Tale Theatre* (still one of the greatest series ever created). I adored Carol Burnett and Jerry Lewis. Old sitcoms like *I Love Lucy, The Mary Tyler Moore Show,* and *The Dick Van Dyke Show* were appointment viewing for me. (By the way, I'm not eighty-five years old. I just watched a lot of reruns as a kid. Thanks, Nick at Nite!) I would obsess over Mel Brooks movies like *Young Frankenstein* and *Spaceballs,* even though I didn't get half the jokes, and loved anything with Lily Tomlin, Bette Midler, Whoopi Goldberg, Steve Martin, and Martin Short (*Three Amigos* was my jam!).

Later on, I'd acquire tastes for more adult styles like insult and roast comedy, and the provocative, occasionally vulgar musings of performers like George Carlin, Howard Stern, and Joan Rivers. Joan always reminded me so much of Nanny. They both had the same playfully irascible rhythm and the same New York accent. They also followed similar creeds: "It's never too soon to laugh," and, "If you can laugh at it, you can deal with it."

• • • • •

In 2005, I found a new comedy muse. I was living in New York by then, dating a new boy—an out-of-work actor I'd recently met in a bar. We wandered into an indie movie house in the Village one Saturday night after dinner. Incidentally, it would be our last date before I'd dump him a week later for another boy who was working as a flying monkey in *Wicked* on Broadway. (I told you I was serious about show business.) Intrigued by the bizarre title, we bought tickets to *Jesus Is Magic*, a comedy concert film starring then up-and-coming Sarah Silverman.

Sarah donned the persona of a wildly offensive, arrogant ignoramus who commented irreverently on the most serious and sensitive of topics, from race, to religion, to AIDS, to the Holocaust, to 9/11. It was musical, it was politically incorrect, it was hilarious, and it was brave. I loved it.

And lest you misconstrue that assessment to mean I think that being haphazardly insensitive or using distasteful tropes to offend people in any hostile, noncomedic, or negative context is brave, you are incorrect, madam! What I'm saying is that it seemed to me, sitting in that movie theatre in 2005, that what Sarah was doing was sucking the venom out of all those cultural taboos floating in the zeitgeist (or peeing on them, if that's your preferred method), rechanneling it through a comedy filter by making *herself* the butt of the joke, and saying, "Here! Release the tension, aggression, or fear you may be feeling about these very serious topics. Laugh at me!"

She was using satire to say the direct opposite of what she felt and knew to be right, which is what made it hilarious. She wasn't actually saying those ridiculous things; she was doing a fictional caricature of a person who would be ridiculous enough to say those ridiculous things. She wasn't mocking race; she was mocking racism. She wasn't trivializing the Holocaust or 9/11; she was lampooning the notion that anyone would. She was pointing out absurdity by pretending to *be* the absurdity.

It was a simulation, like a horror movie or a scary roller-coaster ride. The reason we like those things is because of the blatant unrealism of them, and the comfort we get from knowing that our lives are not actually being threatened. We indulge in artificial danger or shock because it exorcizes some pent-up fear or tension inside of us. I think comedy that is considered dangerous or shocking can give us that same endorphin-fueled release, the only difference being that it manifests as laughter instead of the feeling that we might shit our pants. There's a special kind of release that comes with saying or hearing the very things we're absolutely not supposed to, and comedy is arguably the only justifiable channel through which to facilitate it.

Granted, a lot of the material from *Jesus Is Magic* has not withstood the test of time. Through the years, Sarah herself has acknowledged personal regrets for the actual arrogance and ignorance she feels she unintentionally exhibited through certain bits from her early days. As she says, "comedy is not evergreen," and as it turns out, there are some places you should just never go (I'd later learn that for myself . . . in just a few chapters, actually).

· · · · ·

While I agree that most comedy expires, I would venture to add that we have recently stepped through the looking glass, culturally speaking, into a time when any consideration of artistic intention behind comedy is all but null and void. The multilayered, colorfully nuanced jokes of comedians—past and present—are now being evaluated like cold, flat, black-and-white medical transcripts. People have become willfully ignorant of things like context and nuance. I can't tell if they sincerely don't recognize them, simply don't have time for them, or if it just feels sexier to be self-righteous, but comedy—satire in particular—is indeed an endangered art form. I'm not looking for sympathy, I'm just saying . . . it's hard out here for a pimp. (Apologies to all pimps. I was just whimsically quoting a song.)

Anyway, the point is, whatever Sarah Silverman was doing on that screen spoke to me, and something about the audience's reaction really made me sit up in my chair. There we all were in a crowded New York theatre filled with people of every race, religion, and identity, and we were all united harmoniously in laughter. What's more, we were laughing at the very things that, but for the magic filtration system of satire, could have easily divided us.

Shit, I wanted to do that! I'd never really considered trying stand-up before, but this had an extra layer to it and seemed more interesting. It was more like playing a character, and I definitely knew how to do that. It also occurred to me that in comedy you get to write your own script, which was even more appealing. Maybe if I could create a persona the way Sarah had, and endear myself to my audience, I would, in the process, be able to create a safe space where I could tackle any issue and also show off my comedy chops. If I did it right, I could say almost anything through my character because everyone would be in on the joke. I could let the air out of all sorts of balloons and do magic tricks for other people like the one Nanny had done for me and Suzie in her car that day, and on so many other occasions. I had no interest in telling knock-knock jokes, so to speak, but this could be so much more. I could provide a real service!

I stepped out of the movie theatre that night and onto a new path that would ultimately lead me to my destiny as an entertainer. It would be almost two years before I'd really start crafting my own routine, but the seed was planted. It would take time to find my platform and figure out my style and angle, but I'd get there one day.

Eventually, I would hear from the plaintiffs in high-profile sexual assault cases, survivors and parents of victims of mass high school shootings, and thousands upon thousands of people across my country and all over the world in the terrifying throes of an unprecedented presidential crisis, all telling me how grateful they were that I was helping them get through their pain and fear by making them laugh. I would find my comedy voice—my Scotch Tape—and successfully discover a formula that would allow me to use it for good. But all that wouldn't happen for several years, and it wouldn't be without a few bumps (and a flying monkey or two) along the way.

10

L'Chaim, Mel Gibson!

Working at Cafeteria in Chelsea was a blast. I was really in my element and felt like I was finally a part of the fabulous gay fantasy life I'd coveted for years but until now had only ever observed on-screen. The staff was made up of young people exactly like me—aspiring artistic types with little direction, fresh on the scene and trying to figure it all out. I made some of my best friends there. Every shift was a party. I was surrounded by a work family and patrons from all walks of life—gay, straight, trans people (and everything in between) of every race, creed, and color, all congregating to have nothing but a marvelous time. . . . Not to mention, all the Cafeteria Cosmos (their signature cocktail) I could drink! It was a microcosm of what I wanted the whole world to be at all times.

It was also the perfect environment in which to sow many of my wild oats, if you know what I mean. I was in the prime of my twinkdom and was not about to let these gorgeous gams of mine go to waste. I had an illicit affair with one of the much older bartenders (he was thirty), and my fair share of indiscretions with a few of the customers—occasionally right there in the restroom (only on very special occasions . . . I told you, I'm classy). Some were one-shot deals while others turned into weeklong relationships, at most.

As time went on, my dating guidelines got much stricter. There was a period in which I only entertained suitors with substantial Broadway credentials. One week was a swing from *Phantom* . . . the next was a fork from *Beauty and the Beast* . . . the next a knife from *Beauty and the Beast* (we only spooned). At one point, I almost had a whole place setting! Then I went through a phase where I only dated guys who had appeared on *Sex and the City*. It didn't matter in what capacity (extras, under-fives . . . I didn't discriminate). My biggest catch was one of Charlotte's boyfriends from one of the earlier seasons. (If you buy me a cosmo one of these days, I'll tell you which boyfriend.)

Aside from the romantic merry-go-round of dancing silverware and HBO extras, I was still no closer to my own showbiz dreams. A few random auditions got me jobs in small productions here and there. I played Miss Bible Belt in an off-Broadway production of the drag musical *Pageant* (and by "off-Broadway" I mean "New Jersey"). But I was barely even trying. The obnoxious, secretly kinda true, too-cool-for-school version of the story is that I didn't want to have to work my way up from the chorus. I was only interested in being a star. Hell, I wanted to be an icon! Perhaps some part of me really did feel that way. But the reality is, what was actually holding me back was immense insecurity. I didn't really know if I had what it took and I was terrified of finding out. Plus, practically speaking, I had made up my mind that I would only get lost in the shuffle of cattle calls. Believe it or not, I am terribly shy at my core (especially back then), and not a show-off by nature. I'm sure that will seem paradoxical to some of you as your entire relationship with me is built on a foundation of my showing off for your viewing pleasure, but there you have it. Anyway, auditions have never been my strong suit.

· · · · ·

One of the other hosts at Cafeteria was a flamboyant, pretentious, hilarious lunatic named John. We hit it off right away. Our shorthand of Broadway musical references and quotes from *The Golden Girls* and *Absolutely Fabulous* became the foundation of an eighteen-year (and counting) friendship. About two and a half years into our run at Cafeteria, we both decided that—as much fun as it had been—we were burnt out and it was time to move on. I think the fact that they fired both of us heavily influenced that decision.

Just prior to our dismissals, John had landed a day job as an assistant to one of the top producers at a theatrical production and management company called Richard Frankel Productions. Mr. Frankel and his team were the producers behind such Broadway and off-Broadway juggernauts as *The Producers, Stomp, Hairspray,* and the 2005 Patti LuPone/Michael Cerveris–led revival of *Sweeney Todd,* which they were just preparing to mount. John tipped me off that they were looking for a part-time receptionist and offered to introduce me to the office manager.

A week later, I was in the elevator headed up to the twelfth floor of the building on Fifty-Seventh and Seventh. My heart was pounding out of my Zara interview blouse. I've always struggled with anxiety in general, but there's a very specific New York elevator–induced anxiety that plagued me from my early twenties well into my thirties—until quite recently, in fact. It had nothing to do with confined spaces or any technical fear of being trapped. It just always made me feel like a little kid walking to the principal's office. Whether it was for a job interview, an audition, or just an appointment at the DMV, I knew once those doors parted, someone would be waiting on the other side to evaluate me, and I was terrified that whoever it was would tell me I just wasn't good enough to be in New York and immediately send me back to my parents' house in South Florida. (I am proud to report that I now ride elevators with unbridled confidence. . . . Well, at least I did until global pandemics came back in style.)

The doors parted on the twelfth floor and my heart started beating even faster at the sight of giant *Smokey Joe's Cafe* and *The Sound of Music* posters, and a wall decorated floor to ceiling with Tony Award certificates. This was no Hooters! These people weren't making chicken wings . . . they were making fucking Broadway! The office manager, Lori (who was basically Kristin Chenoweth, plus a few inches and minus a soprano high C), invited me back into her cubical. We hit it off, and within an hour, I was the new morning receptionist!

For the next two and a half years, I opened the office every morning, started the coffee, sorted the mail, and restocked the toilet paper in both bathrooms . . . I was basically running Broadway. I sat at the front desk and fielded phone calls from the biggest players in the industry—directors, designers, and sometimes even legends. Once, Elaine Stritch called for Richard Frankel. I answered, "Richard Frankel Pro—," and before I could finish "—ductions," I heard a gravelly voice say, "It's Elaine Stritch. Lemme talk to the big shot." I died.

A lot of the chorus boys from *Hairspray* would come in to pick up their paychecks. (Yes, of course I wound up sleeping with some of them, but we'll save those stories for the next book. I've already told you too much.) And one day during the run of *Sweeney Todd*, so help me Gay Jesus, Patti LuPone herself came in for a visit. Patti fucking LuPone! I froze solid as she walked through the front door. Luckily, her company manager rushed up front to greet her, so I didn't have to muster the courage to actually speak to her myself. That would not have been pretty on my part. I didn't have an iPhone yet, so I couldn't even snap a pic (which, in retrospect, probably wouldn't have been too well received anyway).

Working at the Frankel office had been my most exciting and personally significant New York job experience to date. I was still no closer to being on a stage myself, but I felt at least a secondhand connection to the big-time theatre world. I made lifelong friends and also got to go to some pretty great opening night and Tony Awards after-parties. Unfortunately, my part-time hours were not paying the bills. I took supplemental work at various restaurants in the evenings and flyered for Broadway shows in the afternoons (meaning I handed out flyers to tourists at the TKTS booth in Times Square for fifteen bucks an hour, which was pretty damn good). With some financial help from my mother, I did my best to keep up, but Mushi and I were now living alone in a studio apartment in Astoria, and it eventually became impossible. My electricity was finally cut off, and my landlord was now threatening me with eviction.

· · · · ·

Word around the office was that the accounting firm that handled all the Richard Frankel shows (along with most Broadway and touring productions) was now looking for a full-time receptionist. Needless to say, the prospect of spending eight hours a day with accountants did not sound like my idea of a good time, but I was desperate. Plus, I figured this was my best shot at catching a glimpse of Angela Lansbury's salary for the revival of A *Little Night Music* (I never did, but whatever it was, it wasn't enough). I booked myself an interview and got the job.

This new receptionist position was definitely not as sexy as the one I had just left. There were no handsome chorus boys to flirt with, and Elaine Stritch never called—she didn't even write. My new office manager was also no Kristin Chenoweth. She was not a bubbly Glinda type by any means. You might say she was more a Miss Hannigan. For the sake of anonymity, we'll just refer to her as "Jennifer" because that was in fact her real name.

In addition to answering phones and stapling tax documents (god, I'm getting nauseous just writing about it), Jennifer also had me keep a log of how much time employees spent in the main bathroom, which was located right across from my desk. She was concerned that some people were taking a little too long. To this day, I'm not exactly sure what her specific concern was. I mean, they were ac-countants . . . how much fun could they have been having in there? I think it was more a power play than anything else. But whatever it was, I was now officially the toilet monitor. I was not happy. Not only did I feel demeaned by some of my doodies—uh, *duties*—I was also bored as fuck.

I had a computer at my desk, so one day, to pass some time, I de-cided to start a blog. This was back when everyone on the damn planet was blogging, so why not me? I opened an account on Blogger, titled it "The Randy Rainbow Bloggity Blahg-Blahg" (for lack of a smarter idea), and I was off to the races. I started writing about everything: the reality TV show I'd watched the night before, the Broadway musical I couldn't wait to see, my dating life, my excruciating subway commute to work that morning . . . it became a daily routine, and an outlet to ex-press my opinions and start exercising my comedy voice (when I wasn't busy keeping the diarrhea diaries, of course). Soon I was hearing from friends and family saying they thought it was really funny. They were sharing it with their friends and family and within a month, my num-bers started to visibly grow. I started getting encouraging comments and messages from people outside of my immediate circle. Remember the Nora Ephron movie *Julie & Julia*? I was totally Amy Adams.

This little bump motivated me to invest some money in my new hobby. I paid someone I found online seventy-five bucks to design a custom banner and layout for my blog. I added a picture of my face and a phony pull quote under the title, calling myself "The Perez Hil-ton of Broadway." I didn't really mean anything by it. I had no sincere intention of mimicking Perez Hilton's gossipy style. My only thinking was that, as blogs went, his was certainly one of the most popular, so I figured it would be amusing to give myself the title. It was tongue-in-cheek—kind of in the way Howard Stern crowned himself "King of All Media." I guess people took me seriously, though, because before long, I was getting care packages in the mail from Broadway record labels full of free swag with notes welcoming me onto the scene, and invitations to Broadway events and openings. I remember thinking, "Damn . . . there's really something to this '*fake it till you make it*' theory."

The guy I was now dating happened to be the editor of a prominent gay New York City weekly called *HX Magazine*. He told me I was a good writer and offered me some work writing for their Theatre section. I was over the moon! I walked around like I was Carrie goddamn Bradshaw. I got to review shows (which meant I got house seats for free), and interview some of the biggest stars on Broadway, like Sutton Foster and Stephanie J. Block, the newest cast of *Wicked*, and the final cast of *Rent*. Once I lied and told Jennifer at work that I had to leave early for a dentist appointment, but really I went to a friend's nearby apartment and called Liza Minnelli. I'm not kidding! Liza fucking Minnelli! I was assigned to interview her for the magazine and she was only available by phone that afternoon. I still have a tape of the interview. My favorite part:

Me: Liza, I don't want to shock you or anything, but you do have a few gay fans . . .

Liza: No shit, Sherlock!

My mother and grandmother were very impressed by my new side gig. That Thanksgiving, Nanny handed out copies of the *HX Magazine* with my Liza feature to all our friends and relatives.

"Did you see my grandson . . . the published author???"

By the way, as is often the case with those bar rags, the cover of that particular issue featured a shirtless, sweaty muscle stud wearing nothing but a cock sock. Nanny didn't care. It was as if she were handing out first editions of *Anna Karenina*.

• • • • •

As my blog readership continued to grow over the next year, I got to thinking . . . I had some eyeballs on me now. I mean, social media was only just beginning and certainly didn't promise the kind of reach it does now. I probably had somewhere between six and eight hundred followers on Twitter. Mine was a very modest base, limited to select, local pockets of the gay and Broadway communities (mostly show queens, chorus boys, and for some reason, a generous handful of leather daddies). "But hey," I thought, "that ain't chopped liver!" I knew friends from the Frankel office had been sharing my blog at work. I figured there must have been some New York casting directors or industry big shots in the mix. Maybe I could turn some of my creative writing into performance and use this new platform to finally get some acting work. And let's be real . . . I may not be a complete show-off, but I've always been a ham at heart. The performer in me was dying to come out. I also had a bit of a new persona now, which was coming through a lot more in my writing. Maybe this was a good opportunity to give him a proper screen test.

I dusted off the old Canon camcorder under my bed, set it up on a tripod in my Astoria kitchen, and shot my first official YouTube video: a light comedic monologue called "Vision Board." The basic conceit was that I fancied myself some sort of DIY, self-help guru who was talking to my YouTube audience about my resolutions for the new year, and demonstrating my positive visualization techniques by constructing a vision board in real time. As the video progressed, my pseudo-positive demeanor quickly deteriorated into bitter and violent hostility, and the articles on my board became less and less about positive things happening for me and more about negative things happening to my enemies. By the end, I added a picture of a bus and visualized it hitting one of my friends who was more successful than I was. (Yeah, it was a little dark.)

To my delight, "Vision Board" got almost seven hundred views in its first week! This was insane. I didn't even know seven hundred people existed! I kept trying to visualize what a roomful of seven hundred whole people all watching my video would look like. Over the next few months, I continued making similarly styled videos. One was about my unhealthy obsession with Oprah Winfrey . . . another about my bogus ambition to get my cat a nose job. My friends and family got a kick out of them, but none surpassed a few hundred views. Enter Mel Gibson!

. . . . .

It was summer of 2010, and Mel Gibson was dominating the headlines. Tapes of the actor spewing vile, racist, misogynistic, homophobic, and anti-Semitic rants on phone calls with his former girlfriend Oksana Grigorieva were being leaked one by one, courtesy of the celebrity gossip site Radar Online. It was the lead story on every channel and around every water cooler.

I was at work, on AOL Instant Messenger with my friend Zach, as usual. Zach was one of my best friends from Cafeteria. We were born a day apart and have always shared a special bond. He was now working at a real estate firm in the city. We spent most days concocting schemes to break out of the corporate hell in which we'd both suddenly found ourselves.

"You should make a video about Mel Gibson," Zach messaged. "It's all anyone's talking about."

Up to now, I had only *written* about topical subjects, but hadn't thought to bring them to the small screen. Maybe discussing hot topics was a way to bring some attention to my channel. Hell, it was working for Wendy Williams. But how would I approach it? Everyone and their Aunt Suzies were covering this story. There was no stone unturned. The guy was a bigoted asshole . . . what else was there to say? In reality, I, like most people, was shocked and outraged, but who cared??? There was more than enough shock and outrage being contributed to the public discussion, but other than one-liners in late-night monologues, I didn't really see anyone getting too creative about it. I would need to make this funny, but how? It was racism and homophobia and anti-Semitism—some of the most sensitive issues you could think of. This would be an ambitious undertaking, especially as my first foray into on-camera topical humor. "I'm gonna have to pass on this one," I thought.

Then it hit me. If I was going to do it, I'd need to turn the whole thing on its ear, and come at it from an angle that no one was expecting. As the Sondheim lyric goes, I had to "get a gimmick." Maybe instead of just commenting or making jokes about the headline, I could implant myself directly into it. I could somehow jump feetfirst into the chalk drawing (to use a *Mary Poppins* reference) and highlight the absurdity and grotesqueness of the situation by mocking it directly, in character. My character was based on me. What could I bring to the table? Then, remembering I was gay and Jewish, I started typing to Zach.

"I should date him."

One "LOL" from Zach was all it took. I suddenly had a plan . . . and a new boyfriend.

That Sunday, July 18, 2010, I wrote and filmed a sketch of myself walking around my apartment, pretending to have a romantic phone conversation opposite Mel Gibson's horrific phone tirades. I pulled the audio from the internet and played some of his "greatest hits" softly through my phone so I could listen and respond in real time (I added the full audio later in iMovie). As he shouted obscenities and racial slurs, and bloviated about blow jobs and boob jobs, I responded saccharinely, with full, lovey-dovey composure, by asking him what he wanted for dinner that night, what outfit I should wear to the party, and whether or not he liked my new throw pillows.

> **Mel:** They're too big and they look stupid. They make you look like some Vegas bitch . . . like some Vegas whore!

> **Randy:** Well, I mean, they're just pillows.

I titled the video "Randy Rainbow Is Dating Mel Gibson" and posted it that night. By the next morning, it had over a thousand views! My inbox was suddenly full of comment notifications and Facebook tags. My friends were calling and texting to tell me that all their friends were posting it. It was like Christmas morning and my birthday all at once. The views kept climbing throughout the day, and by lunchtime, it had almost seven thousand views! What?!?

Two days later, it was at ten thousand views. A text came from Brandon, the magazine editor I was no longer dating.

> Your Mel Gibson video is on Towleroad and Queerty! All the sites are picking it up!

I ran to my computer and sure enough, there were headlines like MEL GIBSON IS DATING A GAY MAN and GAY BLOGGER CASHES IN ON GIBSON CONTROVERSY. By that night, the video had climbed to almost sixty thousand views, and by the end of the week, it had broken one hundred thousand views! I had gone viral-ish!

I was suddenly getting requests from magazines and radio shows, all wanting to interview Mel Gibson's new, gay, Jewish boyfriend. My Twitter account had gone from six hundred followers to six thousand in a week. People started recognizing me on the street. On lunch breaks, I'd walk to the post office to drop off stacks of K-1 tax forms for work and hear, "Hey, it's Mel Gibson's boyfriend!" (Believe me, I've been called worse.) One of my favorite Chelsea nightclubs, Splash, which has since shuttered (R.I.P. Musical Mondays), threw a whole event in my honor and played the video on their giant multiscreen system.

• • • • •

I knew I needed to strike again while the iron was hot. The latest topic trending on everyone's news feed was Chelsea Clinton's wedding, and more specifically, the fact that the Obamas had been snubbed from the guest list. I ripped audio of the president, First Lady, and Hillary Clinton from news clips, and staged a new video in which I pretended to carry on a conversation with Barack and Michelle the morning after the wedding. I passive-aggressively gloated about having been invited myself, all the while dishing cattily with my girl Hillary Clinton on the other line.

Sure enough, I made headlines again! All the gay websites and a few mainstream entertainment sites picked it up immediately this time. A screenshot of me appeared next to a photograph of Hillary Clinton in the print edition of *AM New York* the following morning, with a write-up about my video. (An interesting side note: The cover of that *AM New York* ironically featured a giant photo of then-civilian Donald Trump with a story about his hotel business woes and the caption "Don't blame me.") Only this time around, the writers didn't refer to me simply as "gay man" or "gay blogger" in the headlines. They used my name.

EVEN RANDY RAINBOW GETS INVITED TO CHELSEA'S WEDDING!

RANDY RAINBOW GETS THE DIRT ON WHY OBAMAS WEREN'T INVITED . . .

This was an important distinction that was not lost on me. I purposely gave myself top billing in the titles of all my videos. I was virtually unknown and any social media strategist would likely argue that I would have gotten more views had I given them titles like "Mel Gibson Is Dating a Gay Man," or at least "Mel Gibson Is Dating Randy Rainbow," instead of "Randy Rainbow Is Dating Mel Gibson." In fact, a social media company I later hired for a short stint went in and retitled many of my videos using exactly that format. My thinking at the time, however, was, "If people don't know who I am, now they'll learn." My very catchy and unusual name had been the source of much ridicule throughout my life, but by god, I was gonna make it pay me the hell back now. This latest round of publicity was a sign to me that maybe my strategy was working.

It seemed I had stumbled upon something people were really responding to. Perhaps this was a formula that could actually work. I thought if I could endear myself to an audience through this persona, it would create a safe space around any headline or issue, thereby allowing me to tackle even the most controversial and polarizing topics. This whole YouTube thing was very appealing, too. I mean, who needed to go audition for other people when I could just write my own material, edit it myself, and deliver it directly to my viewers? Screw the middleman!

The persona I naturally slipped into was a heightened, scripted version of myself with shades of the slightly mischievous, delightfully inappropriate comedic characters that had always made me laugh. It was a little Jack McFarland and a little Karen Walker from *Will & Grace*, a little Patsy and a little Edina from *Absolutely Fabulous*, a little Sarah Silverman from *The Sarah Silverman Program*, a little Blanche Devereaux from *The Golden Girls*, and a little me after a vodka soda or two (splash of cran, thank you). The character version of me, as I saw him, was a slightly arrogant, somewhat ignorant, hopefully lovable, part gossip girl, part man-about-town, part vapid social media star who magically wound up in the most unlikely of circumstances, like at Chelsea Clinton's wedding or in an intimate homosexual relationship with a heterosexual, homophobic, anti-Semitic movie star. . . . He was Mel Gibson's boyfriend!

From then on, I posted mainly in that voice. I had an audience now, and I figured they were there to see a show. Plus, it was good practice. I wasn't making my comedy bones the conventional way in stand-up clubs or anything. Social media was my stage to try out material. I tweeted jokes and absurd observations in the style of my character that were politically incorrect and very Silverman-esque (probably too much so for my own good).

I continued inserting myself into the news—both political and entertainment—with my videos. I even wound up with a couple of pretty exciting (if not unlikely) guest stars in my "first season," as it were. When Proposition 8, the California ban on gay marriage, was overturned in 2010, I reached out via Twitter and Facebook to some well-known LGBTQ celebrities, asking if they'd consider making a cameo in my video on the topic. The only one who wrote back was my darling Michael Urie (fresh off his successful run on the hit show *Ugly Betty*). He didn't know me from a hole in the wall but responded immediately and said he would love to! He was so supportive of me from the very beginning and has remained so ever since. Michael is a top-notch talent but, more importantly, a massive mensch and I'll always love him.

Get this! Brent Corrigan, the legendary pornographic actor and former super twink, actually reached out to me back then, saying he'd love to collaborate on something. (Just my luck, he meant comedy.) I think he was trying out his acting chops in the hopes of preparing for a more mainstream transition. Far be it from me to turn down a legend. I threw together a little sketch called "Randy Rainbow and Mel Gibson Make a Sex Tape," in which I call Brent for his professional advice when an indecent video of me and my boyfriend allegedly leaks. Brent Corrigan—aka Sean—was delightful to work with, and very diligent about his memorization and line readings. (There are still four DVDs' worth of unused footage of him in his undies locked in my vaults.)

· · · · ·

My *American Idol* spoof (my first green screen effort and the first time I incorporated existing video footage instead of just audio clips), in which I pretended to audition for the panel of celebrity judges, caught the eye of one of the show's top producers. Nigel Lythgoe, who also cocreated and judged on *So You Think You Can Dance*, reached out to tell me that he and the *Idol* crew had all been watching my video during breaks on the set and were big fans.

Nigel was in New York on business in early 2011 and invited me to breakfast at the Four Seasons. I called in to work and told Jennifer I'd be in late that morning. I arrived expecting to find a whole entourage of people—maybe a few other YouTubers like me, but it was just the two of us. Over omelettes and orange juice, he told me he was casting the pilot of a new reality show he was creating for E! and wanted me to be a major part of it. He said he wanted to make me a star.

"Do I have to audition?" I asked. "I really don't like doing that."

He laughed. I was not joking.

After breakfast, I floated to work on a cloud. This was it . . . my big break! I called my mom and reenacted every word of my breakfast meeting for her. That afternoon, Vicky from the back office was in the bathroom for a record seven minutes and thirty-eight seconds and I didn't even write it down. Who cared??? My ship was about to come in. What's more, I had made it happen all by myself, in less than a year!

And to think, it all started with the horrific, drunken rants of a bigoted former sex symbol. Barbra Streisand had *Funny Girl*, and I had Mel Gibson screaming for a blow job.

11

Goodnight, Irene

The afternoon receptionist at Richard Frankel Productions was a gorgeous, hilarious, magical young woman named Deniece who I adored. It was through Deniece and her dreamy then-boyfriend Scott Porter (of later *Friday Night Lights* fame) that I met one of my best friends on Earth, Tituss Burgess. (Wow, this chapter is so name-droppy!) They had all worked together at Disney World years prior. When I met Tituss in 2006, he was already established on Broadway, having starred in the short-lived Beach Boys jukebox musical *Good Vibrations*, going on to join the original cast of *Jersey Boys*, and now preparing to make his biggest splash at the time as Sebastian in the Broadway production of *The Little Mermaid*.

Tituss was the first real friend I'd ever had with that kind of success. I admired him so much and looked up to him like a big brother. More importantly, I made him laugh a lot. He thought I was really funny and he let me know it constantly. I was still exclusively a receptionist when we met, but he saw something in me right away and made a concerted effort to always nurture and encourage it. It meant a lot to be noticed like that by someone with his achievements and otherworldly talents, and I think it may have ultimately instilled a lot of the confidence it took for me to eventually put myself out there again as a performer.

There were times when it seemed Tituss believed in me more than I did myself. I was his plus-one at a closing-night party following the final Broadway performance of *Rent* in 2008. Someone at the party recognized me from my blog and came up to tell me he was a fan. As you can imagine, this was not a regular occurrence in those days. It was usually my way-more-famous friend who was being fawned over, especially at Broadway functions. Never me. I was so excited to be recognized, I damn near jumped into the guy's lap.

"Oh my god, me??? You're a fan of me??? Thank you so much! What's your name? Can I buy you a drink? Dinner and a movie??"

Though I was clearly only joking about the dinner and a movie, I *was* being exceedingly (and obnoxiously) gracious. Tituss made it a point to pull me aside.

"Don't do that," he said. "Don't get so juiced up when people approach you. You're a star . . . act like it. That's gonna start happening to you a lot."

• • • • •

Well, I kept waiting for it to start. Three years later, it still wasn't happening much at all and I felt like anything but a star. I had signed contracts to do the pilot for E! with Nigel Lythgoe, but the project wound up getting shelved, and I was still stuck behind the front desk at the accounting firm. I kept up with my videos in the evenings and on weekends, embedding myself into all the biggest headlines and scandals—royal weddings, celebrity meltdowns . . . Any male public figure in a PR crisis became my boyfriend. I dated everyone from Kanye West to

Marcus Bachmann to Charlie Sheen. (My long-term relationship with Mel Gibson had pretty much ended by this point. Still too painful. Don't wanna talk about it.) Perez Hilton posted my Lindsay Lohan send-up on his website, and VH1 asked me to be a talking head on a couple of their countdown specials, like the "100 Greatest Songs of the '00s."

But aside from the occasional shout-outs on high-profile gossip sites and very rare television opportunities, the needle wasn't really moving too much, and certainly not fast enough. It seemed like I was finally on a path that could maybe take me to the next level, but my videos weren't paying me a dime. I felt I had no choice but to stay tied to that damn reception desk. How could I seriously focus on my craft when I was on active duty as the pee-pee police at my full-time day job?

· · · · ·

It was early in November of 2011. Nanny left me a voicemail, running through her travel itinerary for Thanksgiving. She would be flying up to Long Island from Florida a few days before. As had become our annual tradition for almost a decade since my move back to New York, I would take the Long Island Rail Road and meet her at my uncle Andrew's house to spend the holiday.

"Hi, Randy . . . it's *Naaannyyy*," she sang. "I'm just calling to talk Thanksgiving. Let us know when you want to be picked up. You don't have to call me right back. I know you're a big star now and don't have time for your ol' granny."

She was exceptionally vibrant, so it was always a little funny and ironic when she referred to herself as an old bat. And though she was roasting me, she was also sincerely giddy about the notoriety (however modest) I had started getting from my videos. She had my mother set up one of our old computers in her bedroom with an internet connection specifically so she could watch them. Most of my views back then came from my grandmother, and that was fine by me.

A week passed and I finally got around to checking the train schedule for Thanksgiving. I was dialing the phone to return Nanny's call when a call came in from Mom.

"Hi, Randy."

I already didn't like how formal she sounded.

"So, Nanny is sick. . . ."

FUCK.

"She was having trouble breathing, so we took her to the hospital. They told us it was pneumonia and sent us home with a machine. We ended up having to . . . anyway, they finally did a CT scan and it turns out she has lung cancer. I don't know how they missed it, but it's . . . it's not good, so they're gonna keep her in the hospital for a . . ."

She kept talking but her voice faded as tears quickly flooded my eyes. Mom tried to soften the words as best she could, but each one was like a baseball bat to my head. I had never prepared myself for anything like this, and for the first time in that moment realized I truly never expected it. Nanny was eighty-six years old, but she still had another twenty to seventy-eight years in her. This couldn't possibly be happening.

· · · · ·

A few days later, I was at Memorial Hospital in South Florida, visiting Nanny. She was in bed, all hooked up to machines. Under normal circumstances, it was hard to get Nanny to sit down, so this was an exceptionally shocking sight. She looked pretty awful and must have felt even worse, but was seemingly in terrific spirits. She was still cracking jokes right and left. And I don't mean your typical stale, grandma jokes. Nanny was always up on the most current events and the woman knew how to keep her act fresh! She was doing material on Justin Bieber that would have killed in any New York comedy club.

I had gone with Mom that afternoon to pick out a rehab facility where Nanny would be transferred after they released her from the hospital. She was in bad shape but there was still no dire urgency regarding her prognosis. They were going to continue treatment and she could have months or even years. I kissed Nanny goodbye that day and told her I'd be back down soon to visit her in her new digs.

Thanksgiving came and went. My mother spent the next few weeks at Nanny's side as they schlepped her from hospital to hospital, and eventually back and forth from the rehab facility. I was back in New York now and got a call from Mom saying that Nanny had taken a turn for the worse. The cancer had spread significantly.

"I think you should come down. I'm gonna book you a flight."

She booked the flight, but I wouldn't make it back in time.

The next afternoon, I got a call from Nanny. My mother would later tell me that Nanny had spontaneously sprung up in her hospital bed, grabbed the nearest phone, and started dialing me without announcement. I could hear Mom in the background asking who she was talking to.

"Hi Ran, it's Nanny. Just calling to say hi."

"I'm coming to see you, Nan! I'm sorry you're going through all this. Hang in there."

"All right, well I love you, okay? Listen, sweetheart . . . carry on."

"Love you, too, Nan."

It was a notably brief conversation—likely all she had strength for—and I could tell from Nanny's words, she knew it would be our last.

• • • • •

On December 11th, just five excruciating, yet thankfully quick weeks after her diagnosis, I was at my grandmother's funeral. When asked if I'd like to say a few words, I said no. I was not brave enough, and it's something I'll always regret. I knew I wouldn't be able to get the words out. My heart was too broken and it seemed impossible at the time.

As the service went on, I couldn't help but chuckle to myself a little as I started hearing Nanny's voice in my head (as I frequently do), giving a play-by-play of the whole event.

"Oy, how long is this damn thing gonna last, already? This rabbi is so boring . . . couldn't they find anyone better for my funeral? Can you believe that *schmatta* they have me wearing? I look like I died and they forgot to bury me. . . . Oh, shit, I *did* die!"

When we left the chapel, my cousin Jaymee asked, "Was it just me or did you guys totally hear Nanny doing commentary through that whole thing?!" We all started laughing hysterically because we had all definitely heard it. And there it was . . . the ultimate parting gift from Nanny. It was by far the worst day ever, but because of the humor and joy she left within all of us—and with everyone she ever touched—we were able to find the laughter.

• • • • •

That night, after everyone had left my parents' house, my mom recounted one of the final conversations she'd had with Nanny in the hospital. They were discussing life and death, reminiscing old times, and sorting through Nanny's affairs when Nanny suddenly asked Mom with earnest sadness, "How will I know when Randy gets famous?"

On its face, the question might seem silly to some, but hearing it repeated by my mother was revelatory for me. There was no question that Nanny was my number one fan. She kept volumes' worth of scrapbooks with pictures and programs from every stupid show I ever did. She'd seize every opportunity at family gatherings (or anywhere, for that matter) to monopolize the conversation with glowing tributes to me.

"You should have seen Randy in *Guys and Dolls*. . . . Everyone says their grandkids are talented but, ha! Mine really is."

I never questioned her sincerity, but I guess on some level I kind of always figured it was just obligatory Jewish grandma stuff. She loved me—she *had* to say it! To hear that it was of legitimate concern to her, as she lay in a hospital bed facing her own mortality, that she wouldn't be here to witness my future successes made me truly understand the depth of her belief in me. It broke my heart all over again to hear, but also gave me a powerful new confidence and determination that still drives me to this day. It was her final gift to me, personally, and it was a big one.

In the moment, Mom consoled her by saying what she believed to be true: "You'll know, Ma."

· · · · ·

The following week, I was back behind the reception desk at the accounting firm, no less apprehensive about my future, and sadder than ever, having just lost my best friend and greatest support system. To make matters even worse, the iPhone containing Nanny's final Thanksgiving voicemail to me had been stolen. I got wasted in Manhattan a few nights after the funeral and passed out on the N train back to Astoria, phone in hand. When I woke up one stop past my own, it was gone. I hadn't saved it anywhere and this was pre-iCloud times. I made quite a scene in front of the other passengers. A sizable dent lived in the wall of the Thirtieth Avenue platform where I kicked it until just a couple of years ago when the station was renovated.

I started seeing friends like Tituss and Josh Gad take off in their careers, and I was still answering phones and making coffee. I got to thinking about something Nanny had said to me a few Thanksgivings back. We were in the living room of my uncle's house and she was drinking a glass of her beloved Carlo Rossi red wine. We were all having a fabulous time and a lot of laughs when everyone else made their way toward the dining room, leaving Nanny and me alone for a few minutes.

"I'm not ready to die," she said with a big smile. It was an odd transition that caught me off guard. She was a spry octogenarian, in good enough health back then, so this wasn't prompted by any specific medical scare. "I just don't wanna! There's still so much I haven't done yet!"

It wasn't at all maudlin. She was almost chipper about it, as if to say, "The water feels so nice . . . I don't want to get out of the pool yet!"

Up until then, I think I always assumed that if you were lucky enough to live a long and healthy natural life, it was kind of a given that you'd just be ready to check out when the time came. I don't know if Nanny meant to teach me a lesson in that moment, but she did: No day or outcome is promised. We're the creators, directors, and stars of our own movies, so you better hurry the hell up and write yourself a damn juicy script because you can't return your tickets when those closing credits start rolling!

● ● ● ● ●

The editor of a popular theatre site had recently written asking if I'd be interested in creating my own web series for him. It would be very part-time work that would pay me crap, but in light of recent events, it was more than enough to springboard me into making a rash and scary decision. When an email popped up in my work inbox from the office manager telling me and the other receptionist that she was implementing a new system to color-code the bathroom time logs we were keeping, I marched my ass into her office and quit. (Color-code your own shit logs, Jennifer!)

Nanny's death changed everything, and not just for me. Around the same time I quit my day job, my mother finally decided to divorce my father.

"I took one look at my mother lying in that box and thought: I'm next," she said. "Life is precious and there's no way I'm spending the rest of mine with that asshole."

• • • • •

I had a new sense of freedom that felt exhilarating and also completely terrifying. Except for a prospective new part-time web series, I was basically jobless in New York City again for the first time in nine years. I wasn't sure how I would pay my bills, or if I could actually make this work. I wasn't really sure of anything. All I knew was, it was time to carry on.

12

WTF Rhymes with Orange?

I hustled a lot between 2012 and 2015. (Calm down, Mom, I don't mean I was actually a hustler.) For the first time in a long time, I did not have a day job, and I was determined to make it work. I still wasn't sure exactly what "it" was, but dammit, I had to make it work.

I was freelancing for the theatre site BroadwayWorld.com now, doing a weekly web series I called "Chewing the Scenery with Randy Rainbow." I tried coming up with creative ways to comment on the hottest topics in theatre news. Sometimes I'd appear as a news anchor and deliver them through jokes I wrote in the style of *SNL's* "Weekend Update." Sometimes I'd pull audio clips of beloved Broadway divas like Liza Minnelli, Bernadette Peters, or Carol Channing and walk around my apartment à la my Mel Gibson–style videos, pretending to gossip with the gals. For extra cash, I did some on-location reporting for the site, schlepping my video camera and tripod around the city to press

previews and red-carpet events where I'd film myself interviewing theatre stars.

It was really in my BroadwayWorld video series that I began to incor-
porate a musical element, and more specifically, song parody. I figured
since this was a Broadway outlet, why not dust off the old singing pipes
and deliver some of the headlines to the tune of well-known musical
theatre standards? It also occurred to me that a lot of industry people
followed BroadwayWorld, and honestly, the thought of any Broadway
professionals potentially seeing or hearing me perform musically (even
just a few bars of a song here and there) gave me a little diarrhea. But
hey, what did I have to lose? I wrote and performed a parody of Sondheim's "Buddy's Blues" from the musical *Follies* (a revival being led by
Bernadette Peters in 2011) to deliver the list of 2012 Tony Award nominees and snubs.

Some of Broadway's biggest stars started reaching out to tell me
they loved the videos. Audra McDonald sent a direct message on Twitter one morning in 2013. It was the first time one of my Broadway idols
had reached out to *me*. She was very complimentary of my work and
asked if I would contribute a video to a compilation she was putting
together for her husband Will Swenson's fortieth birthday. It was only a
small request to her, but it meant the world to me. I've since told Audra
how just the thought of that DM kept me going on many occasions
along the way when I felt like throwing in the towel.

At press events, Broadway stars like Norm Lewis, Cheyenne Jack-
son, and Alan Cumming began recognizing me.

"Hey! Aren't you the boy who makes the videos?" Alan interrupted
to ask as I was interviewing him at an outdoor marquee unveiling for a
revival of *Macbeth*. "Oh, we just love you!"

Before long, actors were interviewing *me* on the red carpets at their
own events! It was beyond thrilling. Still, I was struggling to make ends
meet.

. . . . .

I was happy-houring one late afternoon with my bestie Gerard—then an ensemble cast member of Broadway's *Mamma Mia!*—at our favorite gay hot spot in Hell's Kitchen, Therapy. (There's always room in the budget for martinis.) The manager on duty, Paul, came over to our table to say he liked my work, and asked if I'd be interested in hosting a Broadway Bingo night at the bar. I've always been very good with balls, so I accepted.

For the next two years, I took the stage of Therapy every Sunday night (entering through the kitchen, naturally). I was the only non-drag performer to have a weekly show at the time (Bianca Del Rio hosted on Thursdays), which I'm sure was a disappointment to many of the patrons. But considering my hosting past at Hooters, disappointing patrons was what I did best. My Sunday audiences were often quite modest. Sometimes there were as few as five or six people in the crowd. Nevertheless, I had a ball at Therapy (dozens of them, actually) and got a lot of great experience in drunken "crowd work."

While hosting at the bar, I wore a pair of red Ruby Slippers I'd sequined myself. They were a hit with lots of the drag performers, some of whom (like my gurl and occasional bingo sidekick Bootsie Lefaris) asked me to make them a pair of their own. To supplement with a little more income, I set up shop on the online marketplace site Etsy and sold my hand-sequined pumps. They moved like hotcakes with brides and drag queens around the world, and actually supplied a fairly decent revenue stream. (It pays to be a friend of Dorothy.)

. . . . .

When I wasn't hosting Broadway Bingo, or hot gluing Ruby Slippers (by the way, did I mention I'm gay?), I was keeping up with my own topical YouTube videos. A few had done pretty well, including a sketch called "Randy Rainbow Works at Chick-fil-A" in response to the highly publicized anti-LGBTQ efforts of the chain's chief executive officer. But it wasn't until 2015, when a controversial rising star in the world of hate and intolerance came on the scene, that I'd finally get a taste of real viral success.

Kim Davis, a Kentucky county clerk, was getting international attention for defying a U.S. federal court order to issue marriage licenses to same-sex couples. She was a perfect candidate for the kind of satire I was doing. By now, I had begun working some of the song parody shtick I was using mainly for BroadwayWorld into my videos on more mainstream subjects, e.g., Kirk Cameron (who I briefly "dated"), and a saucy little up-and-coming Indiana governor named Mike Pence. . . . (I saw him first, Donald!)

When Kim Davis was ultimately jailed for contempt of court, I roasted her with a musical parody of "Cell Block Tango" from *Chicago*. In its first two days, "The Kim Davis Cell Block Tango" got over five million views on Facebook alone. (Thanks, Kimberly!) It caught the eye of a few Hollywood managers, including one woman who—to protect her anonymity—we'll call Julia Sugarbaker. Julia (her real name was Andrea) won me over when we met for drinks on her next visit to New York. She promised me agents, and meetings, and TV deals galore!

"We're gonna make you a star!" she said.

"Yeah, I've heard that one before, sis," I thought. Still, I signed on the dotted line and was ready for my close-up! But after months without so much as a cat food commercial audition coming from Andrea— sorry, I mean Julia Sugarbaker—I called her up and let her know, in no uncertain terms, that I was very displeased with our lack of progress. She did not enjoy being called into question like this, and immediately told me she was releasing me from her roster. She didn't stop there.

"I've seen cases like you a million times," she shouted through the phone. "Always blaming other people for your own lack of success.

You're over thirty"—gay gasp!—"and you're still a nobody! If it hasn't happened for you yet, it never will!"

Enter the 2016 GOP presidential candidates.

• • • • •

It took a few days to recover from the verbal lashing I had just received from my former manager. I was afraid what she said was true, especially the part about being over thirty. (My Grindr profile still said I was 26. . . . It still does. . . . Shut up.) I started questioning, more than ever, what it was I had been doing for the last five years. It had landed me some fun and interesting gigs, and I had finally cobbled together an income that allowed me to self-sustain for the most part, but what was it all for? Would it ever actually lead to something more meaningful?

Eventually, I got up and dusted myself off. After all, it was now an election year, which was certain to bring plenty of material ripe for spoofing. I had been working on my act, as it were, long enough to finally feel a little seasoned. To reprise my Mr. Wizard metaphor from an earlier chapter, my comedy "pin" was now sharper than ever, and as it turned out, I was about to confront the biggest, orangest "balloon" of them all.

• • • • •

When former Hewlett-Packard CEO Carly Fiorina, who had been getting a lot of attention during the primaries, withdrew from the race on February 10th of 2016, I put on a 1950s pompadour wig and crooned a cheeky song parody called "GOP Dropout" to the tune of "Beauty School Dropout" from *Grease*. I continued to reprise the song for each of the Republican flunkees, serenading them as they left the building.

My "GOP Dropout" videos were being shared all over the place. Podcaster and activist Dan Savage wrote a whole article about the series, calling it "the best thing to come from the GOP race." My social

media following had notably inflated, and my audience was now waiting patiently in anticipation of a "GOP Dropout" send-off dedicated
to the most bizarre, obnoxious, and unlikely candidate on the stage,
Donald Trump. Needless to say, it never came.

⬤ ⬤ ⬤ ⬤ ⬤

On June 19, 2016, Donald J. (for Jessica) Trump was officially named the
Republican nominee. (I know, I couldn't believe it either.) My parody
called "Ya Got Trump Trouble," an homage to "Ya Got Trouble" from
The Music Man, racked up five million views in only a day. I continued
to follow every bump along the campaign trail, assuming the role of a
madcap journalist and plugging myself into interviews with Trump, his
opponent Hillary Clinton, his campaign manager Kellyanne Conway
(who would go on to write most of my material for the next four years),
and his staff. When *Esquire* magazine asked CNN anchor Brianna Kei-
lar about a viral interview she had done with then–Trump fixer Michael
Cohen, Brianna referenced my video spoof of the conversation, saying,
"I got Randy Rainbowed!" My name had become a verb!

⬤ ⬤ ⬤ ⬤ ⬤

At 9:00 P.M. Eastern on September 26, 2016, eighty-four million Americans tuned in to the first presidential debate. At one point during the
telecast, Trump began grandstanding about his own wealth.

> *I have a tremendous company, I have tremendous income . . . and
> the reason I say that is not in a braggadocious way . . .*

I could feel the country's collective ears prick up as he dropped the
uncommon adjective, and because I'm a Disney gay to my core, and
anything with "-docious" in it automatically makes me think of "super-
califragilisticexpiali—" (you get the idea), I sprang into action.

After working around the clock for the next twenty-four hours, on the morning of September 28th, I posted a new video that featured me in place of Lester Holt as debate moderator (thanks to the magic of green screen), mocking the GOP nominee with a parody of the catchy *Mary Poppins* tune.

He's super callous, fragile, egocentric, braggadocious
Likes to throw big words around and hopes that we all notice
If he keeps repeating them, they might just make him POTUS
Super callous, fragile ego, extra braggadocious

(The *"Um-diddle-iddle-iddle-um-diddle-ay"* refrains became *"Um, are you really gonna vote for this guy?"*)

I could tell it was off to a good start and knew right away it would likely be one of my better-performing posts, but I was not prepared for what I woke up to the next morning. The video had accumulated over *sixteen million* views. Megastars like Mark Ruffalo were tweeting it. Greg Sherman, nephew of the late Robert Sherman (half of the famous Sherman Brothers duo who wrote the music for *Mary Poppins* . . . and everything else), sent an email telling me his uncle would be so proud of me. My inbox was full and there were text messages coming in from everyone I'd ever known. Dick Van Dyke himself shared the video to his Facebook page with the caption *"Creatively precocious, elegantly lo-quacious, clever and audacious, funny and vivacious! What a wit! Good gracious, Randy Rainbow!"*

Two weeks later, Debra Messing direct-messaged me on Twitter to ask if I would write a parody for her to sing with Eric McCormack, Megan Mullally, and Sean Hayes at an upcoming Hillary Clinton fundraiser. After some back-and-forth about song options, I wrote "Hey, Hillary Clinton!" to the tune of "Gee, Officer Krupke!" from *West Side Story*. Debra sent me a video of the four of them rehearsing it, which made me cry, and after they performed it at the fundraiser, my name appeared in a headline on Variety.com, alongside the full cast of *Will & Grace*.

How do ya like me now, "Julia Sugarbaker"???? (Again, her real name is Andrea.)

· · · · ·

That October, my friend Jim Caruso, host of the popular weekly open mic night "Cast Party" at the legendary Birdland Jazz Club in New York City, invited me to do a concert at the club ahead of Election Day. Hillary Clinton was the clear front-runner, so this would be a big celebration/Trump-bashing jamboree. I was totally unprepared for live concert performing back then, so my friends Victor J. Wisehart and Steven Reineke (director of The New York Pops) helped me book some musicians and a slew of guest stars, including Laura Osnes, Matt Doyle, Max von Essen, Julie Halston, Michelle Collins, Marty Thomas, and Julie James. Broadway musical director Tedd Firth came on board and made charts for some of my biggest hits, including the family favorite "Grab 'Em by the Pussy" to the tune of "Give a Little Whistle" from *Pinocchio*.

On November 6th, the night before "Randy Rainbow's Election Eve Party" at Birdland, I decided to rush one final video before the big day. Continuing the *Mary Poppins* theme, I wrote and recorded a parody called "Trump/Pence" to the tune of "Feed the Birds." *"Feed the birds, tuppence a bag"* became *"Heed my words, Trump/Pence are bad."* (A little on the nose perhaps, but hey, it was last-minute.)

I became unexpectedly emotional as I sang the song. The election was less than two days away, and everything suddenly hit me like a ton of bricks. There was this new rush of personal success, but it was more than that. The country was divided like I'd never seen it before. It seemed promising that things would turn out for the best, but the threat of an unqualified presidential administration that had become synonymous with bigotry and immorality was looming. There seemed to be more weight to what I was doing now than there had been before, and it was reflected in the audience's response. People were constantly thanking me (more than felt comfortable, in fact) for using my humor to help them through this extraordinary and difficult time. This was about more than just celebrity retweets and YouTube metrics. This thing that I had originally hoped would amount to no more than a comedy sizzle reel had now gone a bit deeper. For the first time, I really began to feel like my contribution was meaningful. I started to cry as I sang the last line of the song. I debated keeping it, but, ultimately deciding I'd rather err on the side of levity, used another take.

When I arrived at Birdland the next night, I walked through the front doors, as I had so many times before over the years as an audience member, into a completely packed house. I mean, it was standing room only!

"Did the show before me run late?" I asked the hostess.

"No! This is all for you!" she said.

It was quite a difference from my usual Sunday-night bingo crowds at the gay bar.

• • • • •

The next morning, I was on a flight to Orlando, Florida. The historic Parliament House resort (which has sadly since been demolished) booked me to host an election night party. (There's that funny "party" word again. It certainly gives you some insight into where all our heads were at the time.) I had prepared a special Hillary Clinton victory video, in which I sang a parody of "Thoroughly Modern Millie" ("*Everything today is Hillary Rodham!*"), which I was excited to debut for my live audience the moment she won. I was onstage, telling jokes and singing some of my parodies to karaoke tracks while CNN's live broadcast filled the giant screen behind me. As the results started coming in, we . . .

Wait . . . you know what? Fuck this. You guys already know how this shitty part of the story turns out. You did not come to this book to relive all of *that* mess! Anyway, suffice it to say, the "party" quickly turned into a wake. I told the DJ to cut my music and kill my mic, jumped off the stage, and spent the rest of the night getting sloshed with the audience. I woke up in my hotel room the next morning still in disbelief and with a massive hangover. Everything was about to change—in my world and for the world at large.

·····

I've always been a one-man production team, so keeping up with the endless merry-go-round of scandals, controversies, investigations, buzzwords, staff exits, impeachment inquiries, and Fake Melanias of Trump's tenure was no small feat. I was constantly yelling at Wolf Blitzer through my TV to "slow the hell down!!!" The headlines changed drastically from hour to hour, and I lived in perpetual fear of being outrun by the runaway train that was now the news cycle. Every painstakingly executed video was just one "Breaking News" chyron away from becoming totally obsolete. I basically didn't sleep from June of 2016 until, like, three weeks ago.

Amazingly, though, it really only caught up with me one time. It was while making my tribute to the colorful new White House communications director, Anthony Scaramucci. As I was putting the finishing touches on my video welcoming him to the loony bin, so to speak, the news broke that after a record ten days in his position, he had been dismissed. Back into hair and makeup I scrambled to rush an alternate ending.

As an aside, I've actually become friendly with "the Mooch" and have since told him this story. He got a kick out of it. He's a lovely guy, and recently sent me a photo of him wearing a pair of my signature pink glasses. Life is weird.

·····

When I wasn't at home, glued to my television and waiting for Wolf Blitzer to deliver my next musical marching orders, I was traveling a lot. My calendar was suddenly filled with exciting new appearance requests and opportunities. I had a new manager and booking agent, and had begun regularly touring a live show. I was asked to be a bartender on Andy Cohen's *Watch What Happens Live*. Sean Hayes's production company Hazy Mills flew me out to L.A. to star in a musical commercial they were producing for the travel site Orbitz. It was my first time on the West Coast, and I got to work with my old pal Bianca Del Rio and my longtime comedy idol Margaret Cho!

The team from World of Wonder invited me to make a cameo on season 10 of *RuPaul's Drag Race*. When I arrived on set, the producers told me Ru was on his way and couldn't wait to meet me. RuPaul had been one of my earliest and strongest supporters, and until now, we'd only ever corresponded through social media. As a massive, longtime fan of his, I was giddy myself. It looked like the sun rising in the east as he turned the corner in a bright, yellow suit. He put his arms around me and said, "I just love you! The singing, the comedy, the glamour . . . I love it all!" I couldn't believe RuPaul thought I was glamorous! He then took me on a personal tour of all the RPDR sets and his own personal dressing room. I was not worthy!

It was almost time to film my scene. I was seated behind the cameras waiting to be placed. The contestants were on the soundstage, which had been dressed to look like a tacky gay resort, rehearsing their script for the acting challenge that led in to my cameo. My cue to enter was after one of the queens wisecracked, "If this resort were any gayer, they'd hire Randy Rainbow to sing!" At that point, a voice came through the loudspeaker to announce me, and Eureka O'Hara began fangirling, "Oh my god, it's Randy Rainbow!" I would then take the stage to sing a few lines from a parody they'd written for me of a RuPaul song (I believe it was "Can I Get an Amen?").

I was pleasantly shocked by the introduction they'd scripted. I just assumed I'd be playing some random, nameless lounge singer. I never imagined they'd have me playing me! I turned to my friend John, who was accompanying me on the trip, and whispered, "You mean the audience is gonna know who Randy Rainbow is?"

● ● ● ● ●

In October of 2017, I received an email from a woman claiming to be Hillary Clinton's longtime friend and decorator. She said Hillary would sometimes watch my videos to lift her spirits on the campaign trail, and asked if I'd send back a video birthday greeting for her. I was certain this woman was pulling my leg and knew whatever video I sent back would most definitely not get to Hillary Clinton. It would likely live on the woman's phone, where she would pull it up at parties every so often to amuse her friends. ("*Look, you guys! I punked Randy Rainbow!*") Nevertheless, I obliged. I opened by saying, "Hi, Madam Secretary. It's me—Madam Rainbow! I doubt you'll ever actually see this but . . ." (And so on.)

Sure enough, just a few weeks later, I opened my mail to find an official letter from Hillary actual Clinton! It read:

Dear Randy:

My dear friend Rosemarie passed along your birthday greeting video. Thank you so much for thinking of me on my birthday this year and sending your warm wishes.

The rumors are true, I am a fan of your work and am grateful to you for lending your talent and creativity to not just entertain, but also enlighten amid these difficult times for our country. Please know that I am cheering you on for continued success.

With best wishes and warm regards, I am
Sincerely yours,
Hillary

I couldn't believe it! How the hell did she get my home address? Clearly, she called in a favor with the CIA.

• • • • •

On the same L.A. trip to film *Drag Race,* I was invited to participate in The Ed Asner & Friends Celebrity Poker Night, an annual event that raises funds for special needs families. I had no idea how to play poker, so my manager at the time, Dave Rath, gave me a crash course that afternoon.

I was being filmed for an interview on the red carpet they'd set up in the lobby of the venue when suddenly, there she was . . . Rosie O'Donnell ("star of *The Flintstones,*" as she would say)! She breezed past the cameraman and reporter, who was midquestion, right into their shot, and gave me a great big hug. Rosie had been frequently posting my videos, but this was my first time meeting my longtime best-friend-in-my-head. She launched into an impromptu medley of Broadway show tunes, which I immediately joined her on as though it had been rehearsed. At long last, all was right with the world.

After the poker game (which I barely played because I still don't know how), a group of us players congregated in a corner to mingle. Andy Dick, having lifted a few, spilled his drink on my shoe, and Lou Diamond Phillips got down on one knee to wipe it off for me as Patricia Heaton looked on. I mean, you can't make this shit up!

• • • • •

Back in New York a few weeks later, Rosie took me to dinner. We talked Broadway, politics, *The View,* Streisand (obviously) . . . She asked me a lot about my personal life, and talked freely about her own. Over sushi and martinis, Rosie told me I had "that thing" she had when she did her daytime talk show in the '90s. She said I was able to bring light to the darkness in a way that was special and essential, and that's why it was working.

After dinner, Rosie mentioned that she'd love to be a special guest at one of my live shows. A few months later, on October 6, 2018, I shared a marquee and a stage with my idol in our hometown at The Paramount in Huntington, Long Island. My whole family was in the audience. There were lots of technical mishaps that night. Some of my background videos played out of sequence or didn't play at all. But it didn't matter. It was a perfect night, and a memory I'll always cherish.

• • • • •

It seemed the stars had truly aligned. Not only was I finally getting noticed for doing what I loved, I was using the exact same tools (music and comedy) that had helped me through tough times as a kid, getting bullied on the playground and by my father, to now help others through a time when it felt like the whole country was getting bullied on the playground and by my father. This was some real destiny-type shit!

There was so much to be thankful for and so much to be excited about. A tidal wave of dreams-come-true was crashing over me at full speed. It wasn't without the occasional pang of guilt, however, that this surge of success I was experiencing had in many ways (however incidental) been the result of something so dreadful. I would remind myself that this was simply an occupational hazard. The whole reason for doing what I was doing was to bring light to the darkness, as Rosie said. If I was able to add even a glimmer of light to the abyss in which our country had sunk, I was doing something right. Still, it was conflicting, and given the choice, I would've preferred my personal happiness and creative fulfillment without the side of national turmoil.

As the great Harvey Fierstein lovingly said to me at the opening-night party for a revival of his play *Torch Song Trilogy,* "We all gotta fuckin' suffer so that you can have a career???"

13

Beyond Parody

Can I tell you a secret? I've never really liked song parodies. Shocking, I know! It's like Kim Kardashian saying she doesn't actually enjoy taking pictures of her own ass. Contrary to some popular speculation, I do not stand before you on the shoulders of "Weird Al" Yankovic, Allan Sherman, or Tom Lehrer (more technically known as a satirist than a parodist), whose names people frequently mention to me. No shade to any of those legends. I'm a fan. Any such comparisons are always incredibly flattering, but have nothing to do with my personal objectives. I only ever wanted to be Julie Andrews or Bernadette Peters!

· · · · ·

As an aside, I feel you should also know that I now get an email from Al Yankovic every year on my birthday. They're always funny and adorable. We finally connected a while back. He was generous enough to tell me that he appreciated "how easy I made it look," when he of course knows it's anything but.

· · · · ·

To be completely candid, I've always considered the genre of musical parody a generally cheap trick, save for a few exceptions (aforementioned legends included). The long-running off-Broadway revue by Gerard Alessandrini, *Forbidden Broadway*, for example, is a distinctly full-out tribute to the Broadway shows it's spoofing. It's irreverent and self-aware. It's in on the joke. Your run-of-the-mill, "replacing the lyrics of an old Madonna hit with corny jokes about your aunt Linda to sing at your cousin's bar mitzvah" kind of song parody, on the other hand, is something that will always make me cringe. Of course, ever since musical parody became *my* cheap trick, I've finally begun to see it for the complex and highbrow art form it really is!

Jokes and ego aside, when it originally became my go-to device, it was mostly just a means to an end. (Again, I don't read or write music myself.) In an effort to compensate for any hackiness I've felt about it, I've always deliberately made a point of somehow paying clear tribute, both lyrically and visually, to the source material. This makes it feel more like an homage than a rip-off (at least to me) and, more importantly, gives me an excuse to wear wigs.

As time went on, I began to appreciate what an effective tool it actually was for delivering political and social commentary on such wildly polarizing issues. Parody starts you off at an advantage by immediately placing everyone in your audience on common ground. Whether they're Republican, Democrat, or anything in between, everyone loves (or at least knows) the score from *West Side Story* and the greatest hits of Hall & Oates. They're all suddenly on the same team, if only for just a chorus or two, and this can be quite powerful in times when everyone is so divided.

There's a unique sense of comfort, validation, and power people experience when hearing their own feelings or opinions neatly organized and expressed in song. For an audience, this can be truly cathartic, and in some cases, even enlightening. Musical comedy, in particular, can be a great way to make your case to an audience of people who might otherwise be turned off to what you have to say. It's almost impossible for anyone to argue with a patter song from *The Pirates of Penzance*. I receive lots of email from people telling me things like, "I'm a strict, conservative, Republican, QAnon anti-vaxxer, but I just love your videos!" While the authors of such accolades may never be at the top of my guest list when throwing a dinner party, I'm always glad to hear from them. I have to assume that while they're laughing and singing along, they might also be ingesting at least a few secondhand ideas that are, shall we say, alternative to their own. Perhaps they'll even be inspired to rethink some things.

I'm never surprised to hear positively from people you might consider to be on "the other team." I think my videos are a bit like Rorschach tests: open to interpretation. While some may watch and see an outspoken resister stickin' it to the man, others may see the comical personification of a liberal snowflake so precious, he's subject to spontaneous fits of musical outbursts. Hey, as long as you're watching, either works for me.

• • • • •

Weird Al and a few of your weird Republican relatives are not the only unexpected connections I've made over the years. Thanks to the power of social media, I've heard from show business royalty the likes of Glenn Close, Ben Stiller, John Legend, Sharon Stone, and Mark Hamill. I've heard from senators and members of Congress. Nancy Pelosi invited me to perform in a fundraiser. Journalists, anchors, pundits, and bigwigs from the world of cable news have become friends. CNN's Dana Bash texts me regularly. Even America's boyfriend Jake Tapper has slid into my DMs more than once to give kudos for a video. I've partied with The Go-Go's in Miami. The iconic talk show host Dick Cavett sent me a fan letter! Melissa McCarthy called me her celebrity crush in an interview she did for HBO Max!! Barry Manilow was in the audience of one of my live shows in Palm Springs!!! Ana Navarro of *The View* sent me a pair of rhinestoned rainbow pumps one year for Pride!!!!

• • • • •

Lots of people you'd never peg for closeted musical theatre nerds tend to come out to you, so to speak, when you're in my line of work. Did you know that Brian Karem, the White House correspondent for *Playboy*, loves *Guys and Dolls*? (I was Brian's date to the White House Correspondents' Dinner in 2018.) "Stuttering John" Melendez, best known from his run on *The Howard Stern Show*, is a big *Rent*-head. Joy Reid of MSNBC tends to go for anything *Wicked*. Vincent D'Onofrio has a thing for *Mary Poppins*. Jason Biggs from *American Pie* is here for *Damn Yankees*. Bob Saget digs *Funny Girl* (we always suspected, didn't we?). Ryan Reynolds and Tom Arnold—you'll be happy to know—are both into *Meet Me in St. Louis*, and *Grease* is the word for Chris Cuomo. (Chris's wife, Cristina, asked me to make a special *Grease* parody video for his fiftieth birthday.)

• • • • •

One question I'm frequently asked is whether or not I've ever heard from Donald Trump or anyone in his administration. It is with great disappointment I tell you the answer to this point is no. The mutha-fuka never even blocked me on Twitter (back when he was allowed on Twitter)! I'm so ashamed. As for his cronies, Kellyanne Conway has yet to invite me to brunch (though George seems to get a kick out of me) and Sarah Huckleberry Sandbags can't even be bothered to send a damn Christmas card! Though I never heard directly from anyone in the White House while Donald was president (apologies for my past

tense usage to any of you who believes he is still president), a few whistleblowers with reliable sources have told me there were in fact some
secret fans of mine on Team Trump. (I assume Melania.)

A number of ex-Trumpers have reached out after leaving their posts.
Michael Cohen, Donald's former attorney and the target of a number
of my spoofs, just recently invited me to be a guest on his podcast. And
that's not even the most unpredictable press invitation I've received.
Back in 2018, my manager got a request for me to guest on the pilot
of a new TV show being shopped around that was to be hosted by
then–Trump nemesis and Stormy Daniels lawyer Michael Avenatti and
onetime Trump loyalist Anthony Scaramucci. As tempted as I was, we
decided to pass. I couldn't help but chuckle that day, thinking, "My
god . . . it's all just showbiz!"

●　●　●　●　●

The second-most-asked question I get is whether or not I've ever received unfavorable or disapproving comments from any of the composers I rip off—I mean, to whom I pay tribute! I'm pleased and humbled to
report that I've heard from almost all of them, from Stephen Schwartz to
Lin-Manuel Miranda to Paul Williams to Marc Shaiman, all expressing
nothing but gratitude and encouragement. I was even invited to a birthday party for Andrew Lloyd Webber following the release of my "Jellicle
Cats/Alternative Facts" parody! (Thanks again for that one, Kellyanne.)

●　●　●　●　●

Then, of course, there's Sondheim. . . . I could fill twelve books ex-
pounding on every detail of every moment I ever got to spend with him
and what each means to me, but we'd be here for weeks. (Plus, I need
to save some juice for the next memoir.) For now, I'll simply nutshell it
by telling you that he was a personal friend of mine. As fate would have
it, one of my dear friends, Jeff, was Steve's husband. I met Jeff around

2004 at the Broadway production office where I was a receptionist and he was an assistant. Jeff first introduced me to Steve at a Tony Awards after-party for the revival of *Sweeney Todd*.

"Hello, Randy! I've heard a lot about you!"

"Yeah . . . I've heard of you, too," I replied aloofly, pretending not to shit my pants. In the sixteen years since, I dog-sat for him, introduced him to my mother, spent long happy hours in the living room of his Turtle Bay brownstone . . . even split a joint once or twice. He delighted me with stories and insights about his work. More often, though, he turned the conversation back on me to inquire about my process and personal life, poking fun at me whenever my responses got too campy. (Hey, it's hard not to put on a show for your idols.) Admittedly, even after sixteen years, every meeting with him made me a nervous wreck. It always took a few sips of my martini to finally loosen up, and he knew it. Once I finally felt warm enough to make my first wisecrack of the evening, Steve would say with impish delight, "Ah! There's Randy!"

One night, I was seated next to Steve at a birthday dinner for his beloved, longtime housekeeper at a restaurant in Midtown East. At some point, our conversation took an existential turn and I think I asked him if he had any regrets. After a lengthy diatribe about many of his own lyrics in *West Side Story,* he told me he was sorry he never had any children of his own. This revelation (at least that's what it was to me) took me by surprise. He taught so many young people through his music. His work had inspired generations of new artists . . . who told him so every chance they got! He'd been so generous with his wisdom and had instilled so many life lessons in so many of us. Hell, he practically raised some of us! It never occurred to me that he could possibly feel anything but overwhelmingly paternal. In fact, the day after he passed away, in November of 2021, Audra McDonald wrote to me saying it felt like we were suddenly all orphans. I hope somewhere deep down he really knew just how many children he had.

I don't know what lottery I won to have been granted the opportunity, on so many occasions, to stand in the second-floor doorway of his music room, as he reclined in the window seat behind the Baldwin grand piano where he'd written every show since *Gypsy*, and say, "Hey Steve . . . How ya doin'?" It was like, somewhere along the way, I planted a cosmic seed that sprouted a magic beanstalk tall enough to reach such a giant and tell him how much he meant to me. I'll just never understand my luck there . . . but, hey, I'm not asking questions.

It's common knowledge that Stephen Sondheim was extremely supportive and encouraging of up-and-coming artists, and to me he was often far too generous with his praise. "Randy, your lyrics are consistently right on the money," he'd say. "How do you do it?" genuinely asked the greatest innovator of the American musical and one of the most celebrated lyricists the world has ever known. "Steve . . . ," I replied every time, ". . . you wouldn't understand."

14

It's Not Easy Being Green Screen

I'm often asked in interviews and talkbacks to explain exactly how I make my parody videos. To be completely honest, it always feels a bit pretentious discussing "my process." But since we're now fourteen chapters into an entire book on the subject of me, me, me, I suppose that ship has sailed. So here, in ten easy steps, are some behind-the-green-screen tidbits you might be interested to learn about how my sausage gets made . . . (and then we'll have no more talk about my sausage!).

STEP 1: SONG CHOICE

This is usually the easiest part. As you know by now, many of my song parodies are based on Broadway show tunes. As you also know by now, I am very gay, and naturally think and speak in show tunes. (I know, this is an offensive and antiquated stereotype. Not all gay people love show tunes, and plenty of straight people do. Please don't cancel me . . . I meant no harm.)

I have an encyclopedic knowledge of Broadway musicals, and whenever any event occurs—be it in my personal life or the news—my brain is just conditioned to immediately assign it a show tune that best correlates with the situation at hand. For example, if I burn my tongue on a hot sip of coffee, in lieu of saying "ouch!" I will likely bust into a chorus of "Too Darn Hot" from *Kiss Me, Kate*. If I hear on the news that a crony from the Trump Organization has been indicted, I will naturally start singing, "He had it comin' . . . He had it comin' . . . ," à la "Cell Block Tango" from *Chicago*. It's a gift and a curse.

Of course, I've never been above some good old-fashioned wordplay, if that's what's called for. Some of my most viral parodies, like "Kamala!" to the tune of "Camelot," and my spoof of the Latin pop megahit "Despacito," called "Desperate Cheeto" (there's no accounting for taste), are prime examples.

On more than one occasion, I've happily taken the suggestion of someone from my viewing audience. When Kellyanne Conway (you'll pardon the expression) went viral for coining the phrase "alternative facts," I went to work on a parody of a little-known song called "Little Known Facts" from the musical *You're a Good Man, Charlie Brown*. I recorded the whole thing and was about to start filming when I saw a tweet from a follower suggesting I use the song "Jellicle Songs for Jellicle Cats" from *Cats*. How could I have missed that??? Back to the recording studio I went.

STEP 2: WRITING THE LYRICS

When writing lyrics for a topical parody, I will usually prep a bit by sitting in front of a television with my laptop, feverishly typing away as

I watch multiple news channels until I have a solid list of notes, references, and catchphrases on the subject. I then scour social media a bit and make a second list of what specifically about the topic is trending and seems to have everyone the most heated. On a third page, I jot down some of my own thoughts and ideas and start pulling from all three columns to compose a few lines and rhymes I definitely want to include. Then, for the next few hours, I write my lyrics.

STEP 3: WRITING THE SCRIPT

If the video includes an interview section, in which I plan to plug myself into an existing news piece and pretend to interact with the subject at any point before or during the song, I will watch the interview multiple times, marking down timestamps of all the subject's best quotes. Once I have them all transcribed, I'll start adding in my own setups and responses to those quotes until I have a fully fleshed-out script. During the Trump reign, this meant hours upon hours of watching and rewatching all four (plus) years' worth of his interviews. As a result, I am now sexually impotent. You're welcome, America.

STEP 4: RECORDING THE TRACK

All production for these videos has been done exclusively in my New York apartment. When I began making videos eleven years ago, I was in a tiny studio apartment in Astoria, Queens. I've since upgraded a bit, thankfully, to a two-bedroom in Manhattan, but as of now, I still record and film everything in a small bedroom that I've converted into a simple, soundproof film and recording studio.

Once my lyrics are written, I record the song. After a main solo track is completed, I go back and stack harmonies to back myself up. For the first many years, I did all of this myself, using the best karaoke tracks I could find and ad-libbing harmonies the best I could (I don't read or write music, so I would just wing it). As of 2020, I've happily expanded my operation a bit by collaborating with my friend and musical director from my live tour, the fabulously talented Jesse Kissel, who writes me customized vocal arrangements with far more complicated harmonies (damn him) for "the Randettes," which is how we now refer to the background chorus of multiple me's. We then send the arrangements to my gloriously gifted producer, Michael J. Moritz, who orchestrates them using real live musicians (all done remotely, to this point). This has been the recording process for many of my videos since 2020.

STEP 5: STORYBOARDING

Once I have a rough track of the song, I load it onto my iPhone, plug in my AirPods, and listen to it on repeat while I pace about my apartment for several hours, doing laundry, playing with the cat, or googling various body parts belonging to some of my favorite male celebrities, all the while storyboarding the video, shot by shot, in my head. I don't write any of this down because, frankly, I'm lazy. (PS, Ryan Gosling's elbows are flawless.)

STEP 6: WHAT TO WEAR???

The prop closet in my studio is packed with costumes and wigs I've accumulated over the years. Getups ranging from *nun* to *gay cowboy* to *gay Napoleon* to *gay Jesus* to *Kayleigh McEnany* lie in wait alongside blazers and ties in every conceivable color, ready to serve should they be called upon.

All of my costumes are custom built for me by the legendary Emmy and Tony Award–winning designer Bob Mackie. Just kidding, they're all from Amazon Prime. I usually order them as needed while I'm recording the song and they're typically at my door within twenty-four to forty-eight hours. (Thank you, Jeff Bezos. You are my Bob Mackie.)

STEP 7: LIGHTS, CAMERA, ACTION!

For the dialogue/interview section, I stick Post-it Notes to the wall as guides, so that my eyeline matches the subject I plan to edit in later. Then, like a lunatic, I proceed to deliver my lines to Post-it Notes stuck to the wall, which, as it turns out, make awful scene partners. (You know the old saying: Never work with children, animals, or Post-its.)

Fun Fact: I always have a set of brightly colored prop index cards in my hands when pretending to conduct interviews, and for the last six years have been adamant about using the same three cards. They're all beat-up now, but it's become kind of ritualistic and I'm superstitious about it at this point. If they're lucky, maybe one day I'll let the Smithsonian have them.

The typical style of my videos, as it's come to be known, features me framed mainly in bust shots (from the waist up). Lest you assume the reason for this is that I have anything other than perfect-ten legs-for-days, it is not. It's merely for lack of space. Though my latest studio contains an entire wall in front of my camera setup painted floor to ceiling in special green screen paint, it's still close quarters.

Another fun fact you might enjoy knowing is that, because no one can see my legs, I'm often wearing pajama bottoms in my videos. To be quite honest, I'm occasionally only wearing underwear. (I probably shouldn't be divulging all of my secrets to you like this, but hey . . . why not give yourself a little thrill the next time you're watching, and try to guess what's happening "downstairs"?)

My very first green screen efforts, dating back eleven years ago, utilized a makeshift green screen constructed of multiple green poster board panels which I glued together and taped to my kitchen wall. I later graduated to an actual green cloth clipped to a background stand that stretched the entire length of my living room. For the first few years of Trump, I basically lived inside a giant green screen.

STEP 8: PUTTING IT TOGETHER

After filming wraps, I usually stay up all night, or spend the entire next day, editing. For those tech nerds out there who always ask what programs I use, it's a combo of Adobe After Effects and Final Cut Pro. Between you and me, I don't know what the hell I'm doing. I'm not tech savvy by nature, and certainly never studied or practiced any of this stuff professionally. I taught myself as much as I needed to over the years by watching YouTube tutorials.

It often feels like cruel and unusual punishment to stare at oneself on-screen for that long. By the end of an editing session, I'm usually so deliriously tired that it all just looks like a jumble of shapes, colors, and sounds. I have no idea what I've just created. There are no writers, producers, directors, or even crew members other than myself to bounce the material off of, and as a rule, I've never screened any of my videos for outsiders before posting them. I've become kind of superstitious about that, too. As a result, it's always nerve-racking.

What is this? Is this even funny? This is terrible. What was I thinking? I'm definitely not posting this one . . . I'll just show it to my mother.

This is the tape that repeats without fail in my brain before I post every video. I haven't learned to silence it yet, but I have finally taught myself to fucking ignore it.

STEP 9: POST THE VIDEO

Once the editing process is complete, I say a prayer and put it out there for the world to see. This is likely the closest I'll ever come to knowing the feeling of sending my child to school for the first time. (As I mentioned earlier, Trump made me impotent and as a result, children are impossible.)

I almost never read my comments, because fuck that, but my mother, who insists on always reading them, will inevitably call to notify me secondhand of what I've missed.

"I don't know what that stupid woman was talking about . . . your forehead is the perfect size!"

STEP 10: MIX MARTINI, ORDER PIZZA

This step is self-explanatory. (Vodka, dirty, three blue cheese olives . . . pepperoni and mushrooms on the pizza.)

15

Not Now, Jimmy Kimmel!

Jimmy Kimmel: Randy, Randy, Randy!

Me: Jimble Kimble! How ya doin', my man?

Jimmy Kimmel: Lookin' good, friend!

Me: Hey, what can I say . . . I take after you, ya handsome son of a bitch!

Jimmy Kimmel: Ha! You write a speech?

Me: What for? You know *Carpool Karaoke*'s gonna steal it.

Jimmy Kimmel: I wouldn't be so sure, you goddamn national treasure.

Me: Takes one to know one, fucker! How's my girl Molly?

Jimmy Kimmel: On her way in. She can't wait to see you! Save you a seat at the after?

Me: Obvi! Grab me a Tito's, soda . . .

Jimmy Kimmel: Splash of cran?

Me: You remembered!

Jimmy Kimmel: You know it! "Baba Booey!"

Me: And a "Fafa Flohi" to you!

The above is a transcript of the conversation that did *not* take place between myself and Jimmy Kimmel inside the Microsoft Theater at the 71st Annual Creative Arts Emmy Awards ceremony. It's a rewrite to illustrate how I often like to imagine it had actually played out, while standing in my morning shower, staring vacantly at the shampoo dispenser. We did have a conversation (I guess you could call it that). In fact, we were seated together—in the front row, no less—separated only by one Anthony Anderson, the hilarious star of ABC's *Black-ish*. It didn't go as smoothly as I would've liked, though, and while I'm sure Jimmy has no recollection of it at all, it still haunts me.

I had just flown into L.A. that September morning after a particularly grueling week of touring. I was loopy and jet-lagged. I went straight to the hotel to meet my mom (my date for the evening), who had also just arrived from Florida, ate a chicken quesadilla from room service, took a quick nap, dolled myself up, and ran down to the lobby to meet my team, who had a car waiting. Suddenly, I was being photographed and interviewed on the red carpet. "How the fuck is this actually happening?" I thought to myself, still not fully revived from my nap. I was just some weirdo who'd been making videos, alone in his living room for ten years. In the blink of an eye (a nearly decade-long blink), I was walking the carpet at the Emmy Awards as a first-time nominee for Outstanding Short-Form Variety Series, sharing the category with Billy Eichner, Jonathan Van Ness from *Queer Eye*, and James Corden, who was now standing next to me on the carpet. I was not in Kansas anymore, and this was only one stop on the endless yellow brick road of dreams-come-true I'd been walking that year. But some of these were dreams I'd never even dared to dream. (Hey, let's hear it for three *Wizard of Oz* references in a row. I told you I was a professional.)

· · · · ·

I kicked off 2019 with a featured role in the New York City Center Encores! revival of Irving Berlin's *Call Me Madam*. I'd long been a fan of the Encores! series and was over the moon when they offered me the role of Sebastian Sebastian, Prime Minister of Lichtenburg.

"You mean I don't have to audition?" I asked my agent when he called with the offer.

"Nope, it's yours if you want it."

Finally, some stunt casting I could get behind! (Of course if they really wanted to sell tickets, they would've given me the Ethel Merman lead, but whatever.)

Because the rehearsal period for that series is infamously so abbreviated, it was somewhat grueling, but the overall experience was joyous. Having been on the road for years with my own concert, I loved the nightly, preshow ritual of showing up with my Starbucks iced latte to the same Manhattan theatre, punching in, getting into my freshly washed costume, and taking dozens of selfies in the mirror of my dressing room while the rest of the cast warmed up . . . ya know, like a professional. Coming out of the stage door on Fifty-Fifth Street each night to sign playbills and window cards with my name on them, just blocks away from all the stage doors I'd waited outside as a kid, was a special thrill.

It was also wonderful to share the stage with Broadway greats like Carmen Cusack (who stole the Merman role right out from under me), Brad Oscar, Stanley Wayne Mathis, and the show's dashing leading man, Ben Davis, who would become a close friend (and my hero later in the book). *SNL* legend Darrell Hammond had the dressing room next to mine. He played Grand Duke Otto opposite the great Carol Kane's Grand Duchess. They had only one scene at the end of the musical, which, needless to say, stole the show. I could hear Darrell's television through the wall every night playing classic British sitcoms. I assume he was getting into character. (Meanwhile, I was still posing for sexy selfies in my lederhosen.)

. . . . .

A few weeks after the final performance of *Call Me Madam*, Carmen Cusack asked if I would guest on a duet with her in her upcoming solo concert at Feinstein's/54 Below, a swanky supper club in the Theater District. The theme of the show was songs from her childhood, so per her suggestion, we settled on "Don't Go Breaking My Heart." Thanks to midtown traffic, I showed up late. By the time I walked in, there was just enough time for the maître d' to grab my coat and push me onstage. It was the middle of February, but I was drenched in sweat, having just run three blocks from where my Uber let me out. I leapt onstage, and croaked through a sweaty, disoriented rendition of the Elton

John/Kiki Dee classic (which was nowhere near my key). I flew to the back bar once the song ended to enjoy the rest of the show and polish off a couple of well-earned blood orange martinis.

During her thank-you's just before her encore, Carmen gave a special shout-out to Steve Martin. Since she'd been Tony-nominated in 2016 for her star turn in the musical *Bright Star*, which Steve wrote with Edie Brickell, I assumed it was just routine for her to thank him after every performance—sort of like her version of Carol Burnett's ear tug. The blood orange martini–induced euphoria I was now feeling wouldn't allow me to assume the worst: that Steve Martin was actually somewhere in the audience and had just witnessed that piece of shit performance I just phoned in. Turned out, things weren't as bad as I thought . . . they were worse. The lights came up at the end of the show, and I saw everyone's eyeballs collectively dart to a VIP booth in the back of the room where Steve Martin was seated with Martin Short. Fuck my life.

As an aside, "fuck my life" is generally the feeling that rushes through me when confronted with an opportunity to meet people I love and admire. When my mother spotted Mandy Patinkin seated three rows behind us at the Broadway revival of *Fiddler on the Roof* a few years back, I quite literally had to physically restrain her from flying out of her seat and into his lap. I did not inherit this giddy reaction to such celebrity sightings. I become paralyzed with anxiety and immediately recoil from the immense burden of attempting to concisely express my eternal appreciation to the person while simultaneously juggling the pressure of not looking and sounding like a complete asshole (which, as you'll see, is usually what ends up happening). No thank you very much.

I ordered another bucket of blood orange martini and was about to dunk my head in when I heard someone at the table in front of me say, "They're looking for you!" I looked up and saw my friend Ben from

Call Me Madam, who apparently takes after my mother, already standing at the booth where my idols sat. He was waving me over. Another person quickly ran up to me and said, "Steve Martin is asking to meet you." Fuck my life. Suddenly all eyes were on me, like it was my wedding day. I told the bartender to place a WET FLOOR CAUTION sign on the spot where I'd just peed myself and made my way over.

"Something wrong with your order?" I joked as I arrived at the table, trying to hide my nausea, heartburn, indigestion, upset stomach, and diarrhea.

"We're big fans of yours in our house," Steve said, motioning to his lovely wife. "In fact, you're the only reason we came tonight." I don't know if he was joking or not, but that's what he said and I'll be damned if I'm not going to write it in my book. "I was just showing Marty some of your videos in the car on the way over."

"We were hoping you'd do more," said Martin Short, scooting over to make room for me in the booth.

"Well, you know these Tony-nominated divas," I said, taking a seat. "Always hogging the stage." (Another joke, by the way. Carmen is as gracious and lovely as she is talented.) "Look at you two!" I bellowed, trying to fill an uncomfortable pause. "You look like, uh . . . you look like you . . . !" (Idiot.)

"Well, they keep us pretty well preserved," Martin said.

Over the next forty-five minutes or so, I finally calmed the hell down a bit and was able to enjoy some time and a few drinks with my heroes. They asked me about my creative process.

"Basically just ripping off the two of you," I said. I told them how much they both meant to me, which I'm sure bored the shit out of them. Martin told me he appreciated the truth in my comedy and that I was able to pull it off without being mean-spirited. I told him how inspired I was by his Jiminy Glick character and asked him questions about one of my all-time favorite musicals, *The Goodbye Girl.* It was heavenly. He gave me his email address and said I should never hesitate to reach out. When it was time to leave, the three of us did a little photo shoot, hilariously directed by Marty. (Yes, I call him Marty now. No, he never said I could.) It was one of those magical New York nights.

· · · · ·

That summer, I packed up my green screen, my wigs, and my cat, said goodbye to Astoria—my home of seventeen years—and finally crossed the Queensboro Bridge to Manhattan. I moved into a brand-new apartment on the Upper West Side. Once I settled in, it was time to prepare for my new fall tour. I was at a rehearsal studio in midtown with my band one afternoon when a call came from my publicist and dear friend Victoria. I had recently been interviewed by *The Washington Post Magazine* for a piece they were writing about me, and she had just gotten the news that I was going to be the cover story. A few weeks later, on June 2nd, my cover was on stands around the world. It featured an extreme close-up of my eyes peering over the rim of my signature pink cat-eye glasses with the headline RANDY RAINBOW'S WITTY WORLD: HOW A MUSICAL THEATER NERD REINVENTED POLITICAL SATIRE FOR THE YOUTUBE AGE.

The WaPo cover led to some other pretty high-profile press, including a CNN profile. John Berman from *New Day* came to my apartment with a camera crew to interview me in my living room (and also request that I use more Andrew Lloyd Webber material for my parodies). I was also invited to be a guest on NPR's *Fresh Air* with Terry Gross—to date, the greatest achievement of my career (and possibly life), according to my Jewish mother.

The morning of my NPR interview was also the morning of that year's Emmy nominations announcements. My friend Tanase Popa, who I'd first met when he was an intern at the Broadway production office where I was answering phones, and who is now a big shot Hollywood producer, told me there was a new short-form category for which my web series would be eligible. Figuring I had nothing to lose, I went through the process of submitting myself, and then quickly forgot all about it. The competition was stiff and there was no chance in hell I would be nominated. I remembered hearing that the announcements would come at 8:00 A.M., so I glanced at my phone around 8:05 while brushing my teeth. When it didn't light up, I shrugged and went about my business.

I met Victoria in the lobby of the NPR studios, where we were quickly rushed in and prepped by a producer. The interview went great but, as it turned out, I was a little bummed about my Emmy snub. I came out of the studio an hour later and Victoria suggested we hang out in the lobby because it was almost time for the nominations to be announced.

"Oh, yeah, right . . . ," I said, playing it cool. "I thought they were at 8:00 A.M., though. . . ."

"No, 11:00 A.M.," she corrected me. My dumb ass forgot that the damn Emmys were on *Pacific* time.

We sat at a table in the lobby while Victoria frantically refreshed the Emmys web page over and over again on her phone. Eventually, my phone lit up with a text from Tanase:

Congratulations on your first Emmy nomination, Randy!!!

"No!" I shrieked.

At that moment, Victoria refreshed the page again, and sure enough, there was my name. I immediately called my mother to share the news.

"Mom, are you sitting? I just got nominated for an Emmy."

"Oh my god," she said. "Randy, that's amazing. . . . So, what was Terry Gross like?"

* * * * *

After I walked the Emmys red carpet, we made our way into the Microsoft Theater, where we were ushered to our seats. To my surprise, we were in the very first row. Television icon Norman Lear was seated a few rows behind us. RuPaul spotted me from across the room and blew me a kiss. Kim Kardashian's magnificent tuchus was mere feet away from me. I could have placed my champagne glass right on it. I was still loopy from traveling that day and trying to figure out whether or not I was still napping back at the hotel, and this was all just a quesadilla-induced dream. I think on some level, I was kind of expecting to show up to some busted, fake, "creative artsy" subsidiary of the actual awards ceremony at, like, a TGI Fridays, or somebody's house with balloons on the mailbox out front. You know, where they send all the YouTubers, hairstylists, and sound engineers. (Which, by the way, I would have been totally okay with. I love a Fridays.) It was now finally sinking in that this was the real deal.

It was at that moment I felt a tap on my shoulder. I turned around to find Jimmy Kimmel standing in front of me. Maybe some publicist (perhaps my own) had pushed him in my direction. Maybe he assumed I was an usher and wanted to know where his seat was. Maybe he actually wanted to say hello to me. I'll never know. (That is, until he has me as a guest on his show to promote this book . . . <insert winking smiley face emoji>.) All I know is that I was caught by surprise.

"Jimmy! Kimmel! Hi . . . how are . . . hey!"

"Hi," he said with a childlike wave.

"Hi, what are you . . . Are you here to . . . What are you doing? Are you presenting . . . here . . . tonight?"

"No, I don't think I am. I don't know what I'm doing. I just put on a tux and go where they tell me."

"Ha! Right, that's so . . . yeah."

"Is this your . . ."

"Oh, yeah. This is my mom, Gwen."

"Hi, so nice to meet you," he said, shaking her hand.

(Awkward pause, two, three . . .)

"I'm so happy to see you!" I said, placing my hand on his shoulder and beginning to pet him.

"I'm happy to see you, too."

(Awkward pause, six, seven, eight . . .)

"Okay," I said. "See you later!"

"Oh . . . okay," he said, taking his marching orders. "See you later."

Fuck my life. I dismissed him! I literally petted Jimmy Kimmel like a little baby puppy and then dismissed him. I told you, I suck at celebrity-ing. Just add it to the list of awkward, borderline-offensive celebrity encounters I've personally botched over the years. Like that time Zachary Levi—well-known, wildly handsome film and television star Zachary Levi—came up to me at a Tony Awards after-party for the revival of *She Loves Me* in 2016 to tell me he was a big fan.

"Oh, thanks," I said, slightly too drunk to recognize him. "Are you in the show?"

He was literally the fucking star of the show! He was nominated for a Tony Award for Best Actor in a Musical that night and had literally just performed on the fucking telecast.

"Yeah, I am," he said, clearly bummed out that I was such a douche. "Well, have a good night!"

Fuck. My. Life.

● ● ● ● ●

The time came to announce my category. Marie Kondo, the "sparking joy" decluttering queen, did the honors. My name was announced, along with my fellow nominees', by a big, booming, prerecorded voice and a clip of me from one of my videos flashed on the towering screens on either side of the stage.

"And the Emmy goes to . . . *Carpool Karaoke!*"

James Corden took the stage with his team. Naturally, I jumped up, ripped the mic out of his hand, and Kanye'd that shit. Just kidding. I didn't even flip off the camera. I wasn't mad at all. "Not bad for some weirdo making videos, alone in his living room," I thought to myself. I was, however, slightly saddened that America would not get to hear my acceptance speech that night. I don't totally remember it now, but it ended with a loving tribute to Kellyanne Conway.

My mother also couldn't have been happier. Anthony Anderson asked her for one of her Tic Tacs halfway through the evening. That was her Emmy Award.

We had an amazing time at the Governors Ball after the ceremony. While we were there, Stephen Sondheim called to congratulate me. He told me to enjoy myself, to remember every minute, and that I had earned it. I thought of a line Elaine Stritch said in her one-woman Broadway show, *Elaine Stritch At Liberty*: "Stephen Sondheim's approval . . . That'll keep you on the straight and narrow for two or three years." I'm grateful to say I now know, at least a little bit, what she was talking about.

● ● ● ● ●

Now a one-time Emmy loser, I continued touring through October while simultaneously recording my first album—a Christmas EP titled *Hey Gurl, It's Christmas!* Marc Shaiman, the brilliant, legendary, adorable composer and lyricist of *Hairspray* and *Mary Poppins Returns*, agreed to write the title track with me (my first original music collaboration). Marc is the menschiest of all mensches, and has been one of my most ardent supporters from the very beginning. I'm forever grateful for his generosity, encouragement, and even more so, his friendship. (And I'm not just saying that because I know he bought this book and immediately skimmed the glossary for his own name.)

* * * * *

That November, I headlined at the Beacon Theatre in Manhattan as part of the New York Comedy Festival. It was my biggest show in my own hometown yet, and it was sold out. The crowd was full of friends, family, and so much love. Stephen Sondheim sat next to my mother. (She tells me he never stopped laughing.) *Wicked* composer Stephen Schwartz and MSNBC's Lawrence O'Donnell came backstage after. We celebrated the performance and the official release of my Christmas album with a private reception at a restaurant across the street. It was a magical night I'll never forget.

This wild year was finally winding down. The grand finale would be a featured guest role on *Better Things*, the FX comedy-drama starring and created by Pamela Adlon. Pamela (who'd I'd never met before) called out of the blue to tell me she had written a part with me in mind, and that I'd get to sing.

"There's so much more going on with you than what people know. You're so much more than the 'Trump/parody' guy. I want them to see you—to just hear your voice."

The episode centered on the gay wedding of my character (based on a real-life friend of Pamela's) and would film for two weeks in December, starting in L.A. and wrapping on location in New Orleans. Considering the project would begin just as my crazy tour schedule was coming to an end, I was not terribly enthused at first. But it was hard to turn down Pamela's impassioned pitch and the great opportunity. And when I found out I would get to do scenes with the great Molly Shannon, who was also guesting on the episode, and who I worship, I was officially sold. My tour closed on December 6th in Fayetteville, Arkansas. On the 7th, I said goodbye to my musicians and tour manager, who all flew home to New York as I headed for L.A.

My first full day on the set of *Better Things* was the big wedding scene. After meeting my fake groom and running through a few rehearsals with the band, I sang my song—a cover of Tom Waits's "Martha"— for a banquet hall full of extras, supporting cast, and Molly freakin' Shannon. The next scene called for Molly and me to slow dance with each other in the background, which, to my delight, went on for hours. She regaled me with stories about her time on *SNL*, and we had a lot of laughs dissecting the bizarre documentaries we were both obsessed with.

When Pamela wasn't busy directing, producing, rewriting, or starring in a scene, she went out of her way to literally take me by the hand and walk me around set, explaining almost every step of her process.

"Pay attention," she said. "One day you're gonna be doing this on your own show."

Talk about a mensch. . . .

. . . . .

We spent the following week in New Orleans, shooting some exterior scenes and OD'ing on beignets. Once the episode finally wrapped, I flew back to New York to spend my very first Christmas on the Upper West Side. "There's no place like home," I thought. Who knew, in just a few months, there'd be no place *but* home.

16

Viral

Since the 2016 election, the number on everybody's lips had been 2020—uttered more times by news anchors and pundits than Barbara Walters herself over the span of her entire ABC career. It quickly became the magic goal line Americans would ultimately tackle one another viciously to reach. For Democrats and Republican "Never Trumpers," it was the ever-growing glimmer at the end of the tunnel. It was the next best shot—provided that neither Nancy Pelosi nor Stormy Daniels got the job done first—to return to at least some semblance of civic normalcy. For many Trump supporters, it was not only to be the climactic culmination of all those, um, enthusiastic, arguably batshit MAGA rallies, but the Super Bowl–sized chance to reclaim their victory and re-up with their amazing Technicolor president. It promised to be a celebration of the fact that he'd actually managed to keep the gig for a full term. And for the indifferent and "un-woke," I suppose 2020 would be the year that would determine whether or not late-night talk show hosts and the ladies of *The View* might finally return to devoting a least half of their opening segments to more important topics like celebrity scandals and *The Bachelor*. The point is, everyone had a horse in the race. It was the ultra-mega-colossal blockbuster sequel all humans had been waiting for. The four years preceding it had been one big, fat, astonishing, emotionally draining coming attraction. And when it finally arrived, it was a real rotten tomato.

Like some Shonda Rhimes, Sweeps Week, WTF, oh-no-she-did-not, last-minute-plot-twist bullshit, the camera slowly panned from the 2020 Democratic primary, well underway, to COVID-19's black pointed-toe patent leather Louboutin stilettos, up its slender pleomorphic enveloped particles, to reveal a brand-new character with a big, round, faceless viral surface, devilishly grinning glycoprotein-projection-to-glycoprotein-projection through bright red Chanel lipstick . . .

```
                    Ominous music swells

    COVID-19: Hey, gurl! Look who's in town!

                    Blackout
```

In January of 2020, as my friends and I were resolving to drop ten pounds of holiday weight and quit drinking for a month, and making plans for what was to be the busy start of a hot new decade, China was reporting the outbreak of a deadly new coronavirus.

I won't bore or sicken you with extensive detail or comprehensive time lines. If you are using this book as a source for your high school science project or history final, stop now and get thee to a Wikipedia page. To briefly recap, the virus made its way into the U.S., hopping recklessly from California to Washington State, whoring through a couple of Princess Cruise ships, and eventually, like any rising starlet worth her weight in viral nucleic acid, making its big New York City debut! Come to think of it, COVID-19's career trajectory has turned out to be not so different from my own.

●　●　●　●　●

I had been touring the country, in one form or another, since the ill-fated Orlando election night "party" of 2016. The first two years consisted of mainly small venues—converted movie houses, gay nightclubs, and local music festivals that reached out to me personally. I made some background audio/video accompaniment tracks of my biggest viral hits and loaded them onto a laptop, shoved a couple of wigs and hats into an overnight bag, and lured various out-of-work actor friends, with promises of free meals and infinite drink tickets, into chaperoning me as my stand-in tour manager-slash-chauffeurs.

Okay, let's cut the shit. Some of these venues were not cute, and the paychecks were even less adorable. It was great fun and fabulous experience, though, and in 2017, I signed with a legitimate agency who stepped in to handle my touring business. By now I had beefed up my production to include a live four-piece band that accompanied me and my backup videos to a click track (a metronome system utilized by modern live productions that makes it possible for musicians to play in sync with multimedia cues). On a modest budget, the hope was for it to kind of re-create the experience of watching my YouTube videos at home, but in a concert setting. Having spent a substantial amount of time onstage throughout my life pre-YouTube, it was a natural progression. My wigs and hats got a bit nicer. More importantly, thanks to all the content I'd been churning out at record speed to keep up with the aforementioned political shit-circus, which just kept handing me nuggets of comedy gold on a diamond-crusted platter daily, my popularity had grown and was proven by hundreds of millions of precious video views. Live Nation Entertainment was now interested in presenting my tour, and by 2018, we were on the road almost every weekend.

• • • • •

It's true what they say: Tour life ain't for sissies (which, by the way, is how I proudly identify). Even though I was traveling with a tour manager, a musical director, and a band, I started to become familiar with the special sort of isolation one feels when living on the road, and all the challenges that come with this business. I'm grateful for my friends in the stand-up world—old and new—who've been so helpful in navigating some of this stuff.

One night, I came offstage after a show in P-town to find a message from Kathy Griffin on my phone:

"Hey, I know you're exhausted but if you feel like jumping on the phone for fifteen minutes, I'd love to give you some unsolicited advice about touring . . . just a few seeds to plant in your brain about what I've learned along the way. Text me first to let me know it's you. I haven't answered my phone for two years since the infamous Trump photo."

I know from reading Kathy's book and following her career that she knows just how much this sort of outreach from a seasoned pro means to a newbie. I've always been a fan and will always love her for her generous support.

• • • • •

Maintaining my political lampooning while flying back and forth for live shows was no easy task, and I now felt a strong responsibility to keep my growing base fed. I would sometimes do two shows in a night, fly home the next morning, turn on CNN to see what in the name of Christ was happening that minute, scribble down a song and a script, record the track and film the thing with just enough time to jump back on the next flight (MacBook in armpit) to another hotel room where I would edit until it was time to sound check, shower, and jump onstage again. It was like goddamn vaudeville, but in the social media age and without the added charm of amphetamines or Mickey Rooney.

In the fall of 2019, I was home in New York City, on a brief travel hiatus. I met my agent at a hotel bar in the Meatpacking District to go over a list of new tour offers.

"I want to tour a lot less next year," I told him. "It's an election year. I think it's important that I'm home as much as possible to create new content. Then in 2021, I can take all that new material on the road. We can call it either the Happy Days Are Here Again tour or the Here We Go Again tour," I pitched, referring to the unknown outcome of our impending presidential election, and applying specific jazz-hand gestures to each hypothetical title as I introduced it. Luckily, my delivery of this lightly rehearsed presentation was as delightful as I knew it would be, because he ultimately agreed with my logic and said he would get to work on a more conservative touring chart.

Be careful what you wish for, children. Little did I know, not only was my prayer for more time at home in the new year indeed going to be answered, it was about to become government mandated.

· · · · ·

There were just four tour dates on the books in the first two months of 2020. One of the dates was on February 8th in Los Angeles. I had played the city twice before, but this would be my splashiest L.A. appearance in a real theatre, the Wiltern. I was super psyched about it, so naturally I became extremely sick two days before the performance. I was horribly congested and had little to no voice. This was already going to be a bitch of a trip. It was a one-off, meaning I was just flying to L.A. for the day to do one show at night and then turning around and coming right back to New York the next afternoon. It was highly cruel and unusual planning for a cross-country show, but due to a prior scheduling issue, it was the only option. Add to the equation a brutal head cold and you've got my personal hell.

The six-hour flight to L.A. was a horror, and as I had feared, the descent into LAX brought my sinus pressure from a 10 to a 75 on the Jewish Richter scale. It was some of the worst pain I'd ever experienced. I kept checking my ears to see if my bloody brains were exploding out of them. By the time we finally landed, I could not hear. I mean, not at all. My musical director, Jesse, had been on the same flight and met me at the terminal. His mouth started moving but I heard no sound. He was totally muted. As we walked through the airport toward baggage claim, my hearing only improved to the point of severely muffled. (YES, I tried chewing and swallowing and blowing but none of it worked. . . . And stop yelling at me! This is a book and I most certainly cannot hear you.)

We drove right to the theatre for sound check. I was in full panic mode, with nothing more than the newly purchased, vintage *The Little Mermaid* sweatshirt I was wearing to somewhat soothe my anxiety.

"Give me as much volume on my vocal as is humanly possible," I told the sound engineer working on my monitors. "I'm not kidding."

After croaking through a couple of verses with the band, I walked across the street to check in to the hotel, lie down for an hour, shove some tasteless room service down my gullet, shower, throw on my sparkly blue tuxedo, and head back for showtime. My tour manager and close friend of fifteen years, John, was waiting for me at the stage door with my usual iced coffee in hand.

"Do you want me to tell you who's in the—"

"No!" I cut him off quickly, knowing he was about to offer the evening's celebrity guest list. "I can't handle that right now," I said, continuing down the hall to my dressing room while silently praying as hard as I could that the list did not include my lord and savior Barbra Streisand.

Waiting for me at the end of the hall were my agent and a few members of the theatre staff. Having been briefed on my fragile condition, they greeted me with all the preshow optimism and cheer they could muster. I saw their mouths moving all at once, and having now become an amateur lip-reader, could make out a "You got this!" and a "Knock 'em dead!" here and there, but it still all just sounded like Charlie Brown's teacher having an orgasm.

· · · · ·

The show was sold to capacity at two thousand seats. I was now backstage in the wings and could vaguely make out the sound of the packed crowd singing along to ABBA's "Dancing Queen," the final song on our ultragay preshow Spotify playlist and the Pavlovian prompt for the band to begin the overture. I paced nervously in the wings, sucking the life out of a Halls cough drop and drowning myself in hot tea as the music swelled. I looked in the mirror one last time—my freshly made-up face on the floor—and gave myself my emergency, one-word pep talk reserved especially for major crisis situations: "Whatever."

The overture reached its climax (a rousing version of "Cell Block Tango" from the musical *Chicago*, a popular go-to parody choice of mine) and dropped into a dramatic drumroll.

"Ladies and gentlemen, Randy Rainbow!" John announced from a microphone in the sound booth. I walked out to center stage and the spotlight hit me. I then heard what a very warm ovation might sound like through a pair of Apple AirPods after they'd been dropped in the toilet for the eighth or ninth time. I used every aching muscle in my body to appear comfortable and confident, but I was screaming inside.

I got through the opening number (a mash-up of "Let Me Entertain You" from *Gypsy* and my political parody of "Ya Got Trouble" from *The Music Man*), bringing me to my first opportunity to kibitz with the audience. I surrendered immediately and leveled with them. "You guys, let's be real with each other for just a moment. We're all friends here. I'm sick as hell." Normally I would hesitate to make such a self-pitying announcement to a paying crowd, but shit was dire and desperate measures were called for. I needed them on my side. They sighed sympathetically. "It's okay," I continued. "It's just Corona."

Light laughter from the audience

"Not the virus . . . I was out drinking all night."

Rim shot from the drummer and slightly heavier laughter from the audience

Okay, not my greatest, but not a bad ad-lib in the midst of a fever, and topical as hell! COVID-19 had just slowly begun creeping into the headlines and we were all still laughing at lame coronavirus beer jokes while peripherally monitoring its potential threat. The audience and I likely would not have been so amused by my fluffy one-liner had we known such seemingly benign comedy concert gatherings as the one we were in would soon be punishable by law.

I pressed on and managed to survive the first half of what, in hindsight, was one of the most horrifying stage experiences of my life. Attempting to pull off ninety minutes' worth of musical comedy, which, thanks to my own ambitious lyrical efforts, was extremely wordy and challenging to begin with, and without being able to hear the music, the audience, or my own self, was quite literally what my nightmares are made of. The whole thing could not have been more terrifying.

Just then, as I was thinking to myself how much more terrifying the whole thing could not have been, the houselights came on for the audience question-and-answer portion of the show, and as I quickly scanned the house, there from the center of the orchestra section brightly beamed the giant, familiar, camera-ready smiles of two American sitcom treasures, *Will & Grace* stars Sean Hayes and Eric McCormack.

"Oh, yay, it's Sean Hayes and Eric McCormack!" I thought at first glance, like you would if you were at a restaurant and two of your idols walked in and sat at the table across from yours.

"Oh, fuck my life, it's Sean Hayes and Eric McCormack," I thought immediately following my original assessment, like you would if you realized you'd just stumbled through forty-five clumsy minutes of phlegmy, voiceless topical satire while two of your idols watched from VIP seats. I quickly forced myself to forget they were there.

I eventually finished the show and, with sprite-like whimsy, leapt back into the wings where I proceeded to drag my sad, gay carcass the rest of the way to the dressing room like sequined roadkill. I was exhausted on every level but thankful it was over. My team was waiting for me backstage. They all told me it was a great show and that they couldn't even tell I was sick. They were lying to me, which is frankly what I pay them to do, so I accepted the praise. I made a pitstop at my dressing room to re-schpritz myself with Tom Ford's Fucking Fabulous (one of my favorite fragrances if you're looking for something to get me this Christmas) and followed the hot security guard who'd been assigned to walk me to my meet and greet.

On a side note, this has always been one of my favorite postshow rituals. Venues often assign muscly security personnel to escort the artist around. While it sometimes makes me feel like a helpless little old lady, it can also be titillating. They're often very tall, handsome, and "straight acting." (And don't @ me on Twitter about my offensive mischaracterization of masculine stereotypes. Y'all know I'm a basic bitch and you understand full well my use of this highly offensive term as it pertains to the sexually charged scenario at hand.) They're always very sweet and much more attentive to me than they might otherwise be under normal, everyday circumstances. It plays right to my relentless daddy issues and gets me every time. Often, they'll ask me to pose for selfies with them, with an eager glimmer in their eye, like they're so excited to tell their girlfriends they met a real celebrity, even though they likely have no idea who the hell I am or why all these people came to see me. Sometimes I fantasize that my designated security companion of the night would ask to come up after walking me back to my hotel . . . you know, to make sure I get into my room okay. Then he'd take me in his big, hairy, chiseled arms, and like Whitney Houston and Kevin Costner in *The Bodyguard*, we would . . .

Sorry . . . where was I?

Hot security daddy walked me through the wings and down into the small stairwell that led out to the house of the theatre, where seventy-five people stood in line, wearing T-shirts with my face on them and holding *Randy Rainbow Live* souvenir programs—a sight that never fails to fill my heart and boggle my mind. Due to this brand-new virus that was just starting to become all the rage, last-minute guidelines had been strictly implemented by Live Nation and explained to the group. Looking back now, they seem rather lenient. Fans were not permitted within three feet of me for the pictures, which would be taken by a hired photographer, and no touching, hugging, kissing, or gift giving were allowed. For the most part, everyone followed the rules, even all the lesbians who, for whatever reason, are usually the handsiest with me (I think they think I'm Rachel Maddow). Needless to say, the photos people were posting in the aftermath the next day were so hilariously awkward and impersonal, they almost made photos of Avril Lavigne's famously frosty fan encounters look like Santa Claus at Macy's.

After disappointing my last horny lesbian of the evening, John brought me back into the greenroom to greet my VIP guests. There, waiting patiently, were Sean Hayes and his husband, Scott. They were very complimentary about the show and shared an idea for a coronavirus parody they'd come up with earlier that day. "Cute," I thought, "but that story'll be old news in a week." Sean and I put our arms around

each other to pose for a picture and as the camera flashed, Eric McCormack popped up behind us and quipped, "Wow! That is a whole lotta
gay in one picture!"

It was like a *Will & Grace* episode come to life, complete with snarky
repartee! Was this real life or just a fabulous fever dream?

"You made me this gay, you son of a bitch," I half joked as I went in
for a hug from Eric, terrified I might give him my germs but also not
caring because all my teenage dreams were coming true.

I wish I could've done a better show for them, but their kindness
and generosity erased all the self-flagellation stuff that might normally
have later ensued, and left me with only a lovely, phlegmy memory . . .
a "phlegmory," if you will.

I made it back to my hotel room. Security daddy made no indecent proposals. In fact, he didn't seem remotely interested, which
was just as well since I hoped to bank at least a few hours of sleep
before my flight home the next morning. I popped two Advil PM's,
jumped into bed, and stared out the window wall in front of me,
which overlooked a perfect, full frontal view of the iconic Hollywood
sign. As the diphenhydramine and jet lag began to flood the resid-
ual caffeine from my iced coffee and mix with the remnants of my
already somewhat groggy performance high, I drifted off, thinking,
travel woes and murderous head cold aside, this was a pretty kick-ass
start to 2020. Just look how far this little homegrown YouTube experiment had brought me! After so many years trying to figure it all out,
I was finally earning a living doing work I was really proud of. Not
only was it starting to turn the heads of network executives and fancy
showbiz types, it was resonating with people in ways I never dreamed.
I somehow succeeded in carving out this perfect niche for myself, and
was, in the process, perhaps even making some kind of substantial
contribution to a world that desperately needed it. What's more, I had
my pick of almost any lesbian in town. (Listen, ya never know.) I had

no idea where this ride would lead me next, but it seemed certain this was going to be my year in a big way, and nothing—I mean nothing— was going to stop me now!

Ominous music

Slow fade to black

Roll credits

17

*Seems We Just Get Started
and Before You Know It . . .*

My iPhone lit up on the afternoon of February 11th, two days after I'd returned home from my grueling one-nighter in L.A. I was lying in bed, still recuperating, when I noticed it flash from the corner of my eye. The caller ID display said UNKNOWN, but I had been expecting the call and chuckled anxiously to myself thinking of how the person on the other end of it was anything but.

"Hi, this is Randy!?" I said way too loudly and unsure of my own name.

"Oh, hi, Randy, it's Carol Burnett."

"!!!@#^!!!$%^&ASDFasdkfnj;kue93!!!%$#," I thought, trying to maintain composure.

A few weeks earlier, I had posted a picture of my cat, Mushi, sitting on his favorite blanket at the foot of my bed, deeply captivated by the moving image on the big screen in front of him, which happened to be Carol Burnett performing the song "The Ladies Who Lunch" in the

Stephen Sondheim revue *Putting It Together*. The Broadway revival had been filmed for television in 1999 and has remained one of my favorite things ever since. I had a hankering for it that day and evidently so had my cat, whose musical tastes have always been pretty highbrow. I found it amusing how enchanted he was by this particular performance, not to mention perfectly on-brand, so I snapped a pic for my socials.

I captioned the post, "My cat watching Carol Burnett is the only thing you need today." Like most social media offerings featuring cute, comedy-legend-observing pets, it was a hit. (God bless cats; they're always good for content on slow days.) Just a few hours later, I noticed a reply to the tweet from Jody Hamilton, daughter of Carol's and, evidently, follower of mine. **Just showed this to my mom and her response was, and I quote, 'I LOVE Randy Rainbow!' BTW—so do I! Have a grand day!** Needless to say, I freaking did. This won't be breaking news or make me seem terribly unique but I have always been a massive fan of Carol's. *The Carol Burnett Show* was a staple in my home growing up. It was hard to fit in my brain that she even knew who I was.

I can vividly recall, with freakish, Marilu Henner–like accuracy, many of my earliest childhood belly laughs—the visceral, pee-your-pants kind that hit me in the gut and made me realize that whatever that sweet release of endorphin-y goodness I was feeling was, I wanted it all day long, like an addict. Some of them came from iconic bits on classic TV shows, like Lucille Ball getting plastered by overdosing on Vitameatavegamin, Mary Tyler Moore exquisitely losing her shit at a clown's funeral, or anything the Golden Girls did or said, ever. Some were the result of scenes from my favorite childhood movies like *Three Amigos* with Steve Martin, Martin Short, and Chevy Chase, or the holiday classic *Scrooged* when Carol Kane as the Ghost of Christmas Present beats the crap out of Bill Murray, while others came directly from my own budding comedy mind. I don't know why, but I'll never forget a time at age six when, while trying to be smart-alecky and call my mother "ma'am" as she struggled to get me into a bath, I accidentally called her "man" instead. For whatever reason, my slip of the tongue tickled the hell out of me and ignited an hour-long fit of hysteria that brought me to the floor, clutching my tummy in the fetal position while tears streamed down my face. I was so amused with myself, I kept the gag running for two days, calling her "man" every chance I got: "Good morning, man! . . . Can I have some lunch, man? . . . Good night, man!" You might say it's when the seed of my passion for wordplay was planted. You might also say I was breaking new ground as a pioneer of the gender nonconformity movement. In any event, my "act," as it were, definitely needed work. But, hey, I was six and they can't all be winners. The point is, I remember it fondly.

I believe such sparks of unbridled glee in one's youth can be profound and formative experiences for would-be comedians and comedy buffs in general, like losing one's virginity or stealing one's first bottle of moderately priced facial moisturizer from the Walgreens next to one's mother's workplace (I'm just guessing here). For me, they awakened something: a recognition of some secret weapon within myself that gave me the power to view the world a certain way—a different way. I was inspired to find those sparks wherever I could, and to try to produce them myself when they were nowhere to be found. Sure, everyone likes a good guffaw, but I felt what seemed like a deeper appreciation for those belly-laugh moments, and many of my first came from watching masters like Carol Burnett.

Before Carol, Lucy, or Mary, however, came my first and most influential comedy muse, the primary source of many of my childhood belly laughs, the woman who inspired my passion for them and gifted me the ability to make my own, my Nanny. She adored Carol Burnett and was the first to introduce me to her work.

"She had a Nanny, too, ya know. That's who she tugs her ear for," she once told me at her kitchen table while holding a highlighted copy of the script for my latest school recital or camp play. "So don't forget your old granny when you get your own TV show." On Saturday mornings, while running my lines with me before a rehearsal, she'd recount stories she'd heard on a Lifetime Television bio-series or read in a celebrity memoir, like the one about the generous mystery man who lent Carol a thousand dollars to pursue her career in New York. "Isn't that something?" she'd say, with childlike wonderment. She had such reverence for show business and its legends.

The day after I posted the cat pic, Jody direct-messaged me to formally introduce herself. She told me she was a fan, reiterating that it ran in her family, and said she hoped that her mother and I would get to meet one day. This was one week before my ill-fated concert at the Wiltern in L.A., so, figuring they were both on the West Coast, I replied with an invitation to come see me. Unfortunately, Carol would be out of town that weekend, but Jody was all in, and a few days later, she was backstage after the show with her husband and her aunt, Carol's sister.

"My mom's so sorry she couldn't make it, but would love to reach out to you. Would it be all right if I shared your email address or phone number with her?"

"Uh, yeah. And if she'd like my Social Security number and Bank of America PIN she can have those, too. Give her everything!" Less than seventy-two hours later, Carol Burnett was in my ear. Thankfully, the congestion had loosened up enough by this point that I could hear her, clear as a bell.

"I hope this is a good time," she said, as if I might ask her to call back later because I was in the middle of doing laundry.

"It's a perfect time, Carol, and I'm so sorry to make you track me down!" Apparently she had tried calling the day before and I'd missed it.

"Honey, I would track you down to the ends of the Earth!" She sounded exactly like Carol Burnett! I told her I might pass out from overexcitement at any moment and to please remain on the line if she heard a loud thud.

"Well, Randy, I'm so sorry I couldn't make it to your show. I want to thank you for being so generous with my family, but first I must tell you that I'm such a fan. Your talent and comedic skill are unsurpassed."

I was frozen in my skin. I couldn't move and had no idea how to reply. I decided to deflect quickly with a joke.

"Yeah, well what do *you* know?!" I snapped back. She laughed, thank god. I told her the best part of the notoriety my videos were getting was the opportunity to connect with my heroes, and that she was at the top of that list. "I've been getting interviewed a lot these days," I told her. "They always ask me who I wanna be when I grow up . . . Jon Stewart? Trevor Noah? Stephen Colbert? I always tell them I want to be Carol Burnett." It was true. (I've always been very misunderstood by the press. . . . *"FAKE NEWS!!!"*)

"I know we have a lot in common," she said. "You're a cat lover like I am. . . ." At this point, Mushi was next to me on his blanket at the foot of my bed. I knelt over and pecked him on his head as she spoke, thanking him for essentially making this dream come true. He was sitting with front legs crossed, eyes closed and purring proudly, well aware of his magic. "And you're a Sondheim lover, too. I understand Steve is a personal friend of yours?"

"That's right, he is," I said, turning to a full-length mirror on my right to make sure the reflection staring back was my own, wondering who the hell's life this was.

She told me she would be receiving the Stephen Sondheim Award as part of Virginia's Signature Theatre's 2020 gala in Washington, D.C., and asked if I might be available to attend, again, as if I might instead need to stay home and condition my hair that night. I accepted the invitation almost before she finished presenting it. She said she would be in touch with pertinent details, and to let her know who I would be bringing as a guest.

"Carol, you don't know what this means. I'm so . . ."

"Oh, honey, you're breaking up. I can't hear you."

There's a new level of hatred you discover for AT&T when your service fucks up a call with an iconic national treasure—an outer realm you visit that harbors a panicked rage different from the kind you might well know from the typical choppy FaceTime with your friend or dropped call with a long-awaited customer service representative. It's hot and it burns. I quickly ran out of my bedroom, down the hall to the studio room where I film all my videos, desperately searching for service.

My studio is decorated cheerfully. There's a rainbow-colored rug from CB2 on the floor, below lots of light stands, tripods, and other sound and video equipment. One wall is coated in a bright lime-green, professional-grade chroma key (or green screen) paint, and the others are adorned with memorabilia representing stuff that's inspired me since childhood: window cards from Broadway shows like *Rent*, *Sweeney Todd*, and the Jerry Lewis revival of *Damn Yankees*; a rare series of promotional posters for Shelley Duvall's star-studded 1980s television anthology *Faerie Tale Theatre*; framed album covers of recordings like the Judy Garland Carnegie Hall concert and original cast recording of *The Wiz* . . . (You get the point: I'm even gayer than you thought.) Above the window is a brightly painted sign I found on sale at a Michaels craft store that says PLAYROOM (my mission statement for the space), and perched on the windowsill are various tchotchkes and Funko Pop! figurines of Care Bears and horror movie villains (also a fake fan-made Funko of me), along with leaning picture frames housing things like an old *Time* magazine cover celebrating the opening of Disney World, a vintage ad for *Mary Poppins*, and an 8x10 of Carol Burnett in her twenties. Next to that, a black-and-white canvas print of a photo of me and Nanny taken some Thanksgiving, which my aunt Janis gave me the night I played the Beacon Theatre in New York. Now, having found a restored phone connection, I also found myself serendipitously planted directly in front of it.

"Carol, before I let you go, I just have to tell you that I had a Nanny, too. Her name was Irene and she loved you." My eyes were shut tight now and I was speaking determinedly as though I were reciting the Torah, afraid I might never have the chance to speak to her again. "I know she's smiling down on us having this conversation now." Carol told me it meant the world to her and that she loved me. My eyes were open again and I was looking at the black-and-white Thanksgiving photo, thinking, "Isn't that something, Nanny?"

I hung up and immediately called my mother to relay every detail of what had just happened. She started laughing ecstatically, the kind of giddy, borderline-cry laughter I can hear coming directly from her heart anytime something great happens to me. We talked about what Nanny would think. Then I told her we'd been invited to the Sondheim Award Gala in April (my mom's birthday month, and also Carol's). After a quick freak-out session, a few more heart laughs, and a brief, preliminary brainstorm about booking her flight and what she might wear, she hung up on me to ride through town like the Paul Revere of South Florida, alerting all her friends and family.

I assumed the invitation from Carol would be followed by some formal, impersonal outreach by an assistant she would likely send in to iron out all the minutiae of scheduling and ticket details. I mean, that's totally what my move would've been and I'm not even Carol Burnett yet. To my delight, however, two days later there was a voicemail in my inbox from her, personally, saying she had some more information about the event and that she hoped I could still make it. I called back and she picked right up.

"Hi, darling, I just watched your latest!" she told me, referring to my newest video, a parody of the electropop 2017 chart-topper "New Rules" by Dua Lipa, which I had literally posted an hour before returning her call. I thanked her, half-flattered by her zealous enthusiasm and half deeply ashamed, silently calculating all the times I cursed in the video and knowing she likely had no idea who Dua Lipa was. Hell, I barely knew.

I told her nothing could stop me from attending the gala, at which point she began running through the evening's tentative itinerary: cocktails, dinner, entertainment . . .

"Then I'll get up and give a little speech, and be terrified."

"You?" I said, genuinely shocked. "But they throw awards at you every time you leave the house. Don't tell me you still get scared at these things."

"Oh, yes, you never get used to that." Clearly, all her years as a legend have made her no less gracious or modest when it comes to accolades (one thing we do not share; I've already cleared a shelf for the Pulitzer medal this book will surely win me).

She ran through the short list of attendees who would be sitting at our table, which included herself, David Crane who created the sitcom *Friends*, me and my mother . . . ya know, all the Hollywood big shots. I was thrilled. I'd just assumed I would be at a separate table near the kitchen and maybe, if I was lucky, get to introduce my mom to her on her way in or out. Now, not only was I going to sit with the guest of honor at her own table, I was likely a shoo-in for the role of Rachel in the inevitable reboot of *Friends*!

Knowing I'd be interested, she then shifted the conversation to some relevant reminiscence about her "old show," as she referred to it, recalling a sketch in which she and famous opera stars Eileen Farrell and Marilyn Horne sang a Sondheim tribute dressed as the Andrews Sisters. At this point, I had sprouted fairy wings and begun to levitate.

I was standing outside the 7-Eleven attached to my apartment building and passersby undoubtedly were wondering why beams of light were suddenly bursting off my body. I interjected questions when I had them and she was more than happy to oblige my curiosity. It was like my very own private *Carol Burnett Show* Q&A! I debated requesting a Tarzan yell but ultimately decided not to push it.

"This is going to be such fun!" she said of our upcoming date night.

Three weeks later, I was on the phone with my agent. News of COVID-19 was now front and center. He told me that all of the fall tour dates we were preparing to announce, including my own evening at The Kennedy Center and a potential limited one-man engagement on Broadway, were now up in the air. We would have to hold off on making any announcements as the powers that be continued to monitor the rapidly changing situation. All other events around the world, both large and small, would soon follow suit. That same night, an email from Carol:

> Hi Dear One,
>
> The Sondheim Gala has been postponed to June 29th due to the coronavirus. A wise decision. I hope you and your mom will be available on this later date.
>
> Sending you tons of love.
> C

I thought, how could a virus whose name meant "crown" be so cruel to a lovable queen like me? All the bustle and joy of the previous weeks had deflated in almost an instant. A state of emergency had been declared in New York. Broadway had gone dark, indefinitely (an historic event in itself). Soon, all schools and nonessential businesses like salons and bars would be shut down, making two of the first casualties of this crisis my hair and my social life, and Governor Andrew Cuomo would order all citizens of the state to self-quarantine inside their homes. With all my business and social prospects now on hold, there was nothing to do but sit home by myself, google symptoms frantically, and wait.

At least I had my cat. . . .

18

...Comes the Time
We Have to Say So Long

When the *Titanic* hit the iceberg on April 15th of 1912, legend has it that the eight band members on board assembled in the first-class lounge and performed in an effort to keep everyone calm. As the ship continued to plunge into the North Atlantic, they moved to the forward half of the deck and continued playing until the ship sank. I must say, I've always felt somewhat simpatico with those guys. When America first hit an iceberg—a great big, bloated, orange asshole of an iceberg—in 2016, I picked up my violin, so to speak, and started playing while most rational people were fucking panicking. By March of 2020, America had struck a second iceberg in the form of a global pandemic, and though I was scared shitless and just about ready to jump ship, something told me it was time to hit the deck and play faster and louder than ever before. "Where is he going with this self-important historical analogy," you ask? I don't know, but James Cameron had better take note. (*Randy: The Movie*? Call me, Jim.)

Truth be told, I think it was all those thank-you's I'd received from people at meet and greets and on social media, echoing in my ear. They were so grateful for some comedic respite, I couldn't let them down now when I knew they'd need it more than ever. And trust me, I was grateful for the opportunity to provide it. The start of the pandemic brought on something of an epiphany for me. I realized how much the work I'd been doing was holding *me* together through these tough times. I've long suffered from depression and anxiety. To have the gift of distraction in the form of a creative outlet that allowed me to not only play dress-up and have a marvelous time doing what I loved, but also express some of the angst I was feeling about the world at large, was immensely cathartic.

There was no more touring, no more schlepping, no more moving, shaking, or even casual socializing. I was finally living in Manhattan, just like I'd always dreamed. The incredible skyline surrounding my new Upper West Side apartment was almost an exact, real-life replica of the mural my friend Evyan had painted on my bedroom wall back during my high school days in Florida. But it might as well have still been a mural. New York City had become the epicenter of the virus and was completely shut down. I, like so many, was petrified. I would ultimately isolate in my apartment for months, too panicked to even take the elevator down to collect my mail.

The whirlwind I had been swept up in for the past four years suddenly came to a screeching halt and dropped me right where I'd started. I was home alone with nothing but my video camera, my green screen, my MacBook, a well-stocked costume closet, and my cat Mushi. And little Mushi wasn't in top form. He had recently turned seventeen and was diagnosed with early-stage kidney disease on a visit to the vet earlier that month. They prescribed daily fluid injections to keep him hydrated, which I was instructed to administer myself. This alone was traumatic for me, as I've never been good with handling needles.

(I don't even sew my own gowns.) "You're my only pandemic buddy, kiddo," I told him. "Don't you get sick on me now. We got this."

• • • • •

Production on every major film and television set had stopped, but thanks to my highly self-contained operation, I was able to carry on business as usual. News coverage and discussion of the upcoming presidential election had all but evaporated and suddenly my satire had a horrible new star: COVID-19. I set all our newfound fears and frustrations to song in my first pandemic-themed video called "The Coronavirus Lament," a parody of "Adelaide's Lament" from *Guys and Dolls*.

> *You can spray all the hand sanitizer wherever the virus lurks*
> *But good luck finding any on Amazon or Bath and Body Works*
> *If the experts assembled to save you are led by a bunch of jerks*
> *A person . . . could develop a cold . . .*

My follow-up was called "Social Distance," a tribute to the trendy new catchphrase inspired by the CDC's latest guidelines, set to the tune of "Go the Distance" from Disney's *Hercules*. While recording the song, I had to keep pausing because the sound of ambulance sirens outside the window in my home studio was so horrifically constant. New York City seemed almost like a war zone. It was a scene out of a postapocalyptic sci-fi movie, and there I was in the middle of it, singing Disney power ballads. "What the fuck am I doing?" I thought.

• • • • •

Speaking of "what the fuck," that was the general reaction most of us had to the leadership (or lack thereof) coming from the White House during this chaotic time. Our fake president seemed more interested in his own photo ops than our general safety, and would soon go on to famously opine, live on national television, that injecting a person with bleach and sunshine might cure them of this deadly virus. Most Americans were frightened, vulnerable, and in need of a daddy. Enter New York Governor Andrew Cuomo.

Until now, I admittedly had never formed much of an opinion about my own governor. I of course knew he was a polarizing figure like most political leaders, but my interests in the Cuomo bloodline to this point had been fairly limited to googling images of Chris's wet T-shirt hurricane coverage. Andrew Cuomo was now being widely lauded for his measured, informative, and compassionate daily press briefings. The mainstream media were referring to him as the anti-Trump, while late-night talk show hosts and adoring fans had begun to come out officially as "Cuomosexuals," a new moniker gaining traction on social media. (Urban Dictionary would eventually credit me with popularizing the term, but I did not coin it.) Foes and allies alike were praising him, right and left. Some had even begun fantasizing about a possible 2020 presidential run.

I, on the other hand, was picking out costumes. I wrote a parody song called "Andy!" to the tune of "Sandy" from the film version of *Grease*. I dressed in a Danny Zuko pompadour and leather jacket to belt out the corny love song, backing myself up doo-wop style in a Pink Ladies jacket and matching pink wig. *"Oh Andy, baby, you're so strong and rational,"* I sang with all the googly-eyed fervor of a horny, lovesick 1950s teenager. *"From now on I identify as Cuomosexual."*

After years of acting out dysfunctional relationships with the likes of Mel Gibson and Anthony Weiner, and criticizing the bad behavior of Trump and his minions, this was perhaps the most positive message I'd ever delivered to a politician who I felt was actually treating me right. You might say it was my healthiest public relationship with a man to date. (And boy, would it come back to bite me on the ass.)

The video went viral and was trending on Twitter almost instantly.

Still, I wouldn't fully realize the impact it had until months later when Andrew Cuomo himself wrote about me and my video in his book *American Crisis*. I also wouldn't realize how much I would henceforth be known to the press and public as the official mascot and spokesperson of Cuomosexuals everywhere until shit really started hitting the fan for ol' Andy. (More on that later.)

Initial response to the video was generally as positive and light-hearted as the spirit in which it was intended. Sarah Silverman tweeted it with a warning to Chelsea Handler, who had been very public about her romantic interest in Cuomo (to be taken with a grain of comedy salt, I'm sure), that she now had some competition in me. My sister-wife Cristina Cuomo (actual wife of Chris) called to interview me for her magazine *The Purist*.

"Chris wanted to get on the phone and say hi," she told me at the end of our chat, "but he had to take our son fishing."

"Oh, I'll wait," I assured her, but apparently she had to "take another call." Whatever.

I was even approached by a reputable publisher with an offer to write a whole novelty book about my love of Andrew Cuomo. (Thank you lord Jesus for granting me the wisdom and foresight to turn that one down.) Of course, there was also some immediate backlash. Many people who had justifiably been questioning Cuomo's handling of nursing homes at the start of the pandemic (an emerging controversy on which I was not well versed at the time) criticized me for "deifying" him.

Here's the thing: While in reality I 100 percent count myself among the millions of New Yorkers and Americans who sincerely appreciated his leadership during that time, my "Andy!" parody—the video in which I dressed as a Pink Lady and sang, in character, a song from the musical *Grease*—was not really intended as a personal testimony, and certainly not a solemn endorsement of all the man's political or personal actions, past, present, and future. Like most of my work, it was a caricatured snapshot of a specific cultural moment in time, not to be regarded as comprehensive journalism (I figured the wigs and show tunes were a tip-off). While it was undoubtedly a tribute in large part, it was just as much a tongue-in-cheek roast of all those thirsty, penned-up-by-Covid Cuomo fans (myself included) who were suddenly jizzing all over "The Love Gov."

●　●　●　●　●

The social media craze my new video had sparked continued for days, and the reviews kept pouring in, but I soon had to hit pause because something bigger and sadder was unfolding for me personally. Just about thirty-six hours after the video was posted, Mushi, whose health had seemingly begun to improve, took an abrupt turn for the worse. Late that night, he hopped off the bed to use the litter box in the next room. After ten minutes had passed, I went to check on him and found him standing in the hallway. He was hunched over, midstep, as if he'd been zapped by Mr. Freeze's cryogenic freeze gun from *Batman*. I got down on the floor trying to encourage him to walk, but he wouldn't budge. He was blinking and breathing but otherwise looked like taxidermy. I'd never seen anything like it and was freaking out. After twenty minutes or so, I picked him up and moved him to his favorite spot on the bed, where he eventually rolled onto his side and went to sleep.

The next morning, he was moving very slowly. He jumped off the bed and slumped down onto his side as quickly as his paws hit the floor. I called the animal hospital once it opened. This was early April of 2020—the very beginning of the pandemic. New Yorkers were still being advised to shelter in place, and I was still scared to leave my apartment. Hell, at that point, many of us were too scared to even open our windows. The vet told me they weren't allowing people into the facility and recommended a special pet transportation service to drive him there and back. I put him in his carrier and sat with him by the front door until his pickup arrived.

The vet called thirty minutes later to let me know that his kidney disease had advanced considerably, and that he'd lost another full pound since our last visit. She was sending him home with a giant bundle of meds.

"We're gonna give this our best shot," she said. "We have to try and get him to eat. I would give it a full week, and then I'm afraid you might have a tough decision to make."

"This can't be happening," I told myself. "Not now."

I sat on the floor with him in the hallway as he slept later that night, petting him and crying. "We got this, Mushi." I kept repeating that to him like a mantra—"We got this . . . We got this . . ." I was so terrified of what might happen in the next few days, I just wanted him to know that no matter what, he wouldn't be alone. I think I also probably wanted *me* to know that, somehow, neither would I. My phone, which was sitting next to me on the floor, suddenly lit up with a notification from Cameo (the site where fans reach out to public people and request personalized video messages for their friends' birthdays or other occasions). I ignored it at first, but always on the lookout for cosmic signs in times like these, picked up the phone and read. A new request had come in from a man whose wife had just been diagnosed with cancer. "She loves you and your videos so much," the man wrote. "A message from you would really help to lift her spirits. My wife's name is Nani, pronounced like 'Nanny.'" A warm wave of relief washed over me. I knew whatever happened, someone was looking out for us. "We got this, Mush," I whispered again.

(P.S.—That man's wife got an extremely lengthy and emotional Cameo video back from me the next day. It was like twelve minutes long. I'm sure they both thought I was a lunatic.)

* * * * *

A few days had passed. Despite my most creative culinary efforts, Mushi had still not eaten a bite and his condition had visibly worsened. He was now stumbling around and falling over like an old man just before last call at the pub. That Easter Sunday, I woke up to find him in the bathroom, wobbling in a pool of his urine. He was confused and he was clearly suffering. His once strong, full body and thick, shiny coat now looked like a skeleton covered in wispy patches of fur. After a series of highly dramatic and emotional breakdowns throughout the day (which I've no doubt Sally Field will reenact flawlessly in the film version), I finally came to the decision that it was time to let my boy go.

He could barely open his eyes now and could no longer climb his steps to his favorite spot on my bed. I put a blanket on the floor in my bedroom which I laid him on, and I lay down next to him for what I knew would be our last night together. I ran through all his most prestigious achievements and told him he should be proud of what he'd accomplished in his little life. After all, not many cats had been profiled on CNN, or written about in *The New York Times* AND *The Washington Post*. I told him stories about old times—how we first met seventeen years ago in that little Astoria pet shop on Steinway Street. I sang to him. The first song that came to mind was "Somewhere Only We Know" by the band Keane. I had been listening to it a lot that week and thinking about my early days in New York. I'd grown up so much since coming to Manhattan in 2002 and lived what felt like at least nine lives of my own. There was only one other little soul by my side through it all . . . good times and bum times, crappy apartments, crazy roommates, old boyfriends, fleas, bedbugs, blackouts, Donald Trump . . . The work I'd been doing over the last decade required me to isolate so much that having him there, especially during those lonely, all-night editing sessions, made all the difference. I had lost pets before, but this was a special and significant bond.

• • • • •

The next morning was appropriately gray and stormy. I called the vet and told her it was time.

"We still can't let anyone in," she reminded me. "We're unfortunately having people say goodbye to their pets out on the street."

She recommended using the pet transportation service again, but I couldn't bear sending him back with a stranger. Not this time. God bless my friend Ben from the production of *Call Me Madam* I'd done at City Center the year before, who I called in hysterics. He rented a car and was on his way over.

• • • • •

Of course we always volunteer ourselves for this inevitable heartbreak when we bring pets into our lives. I had been dreading this day for seventeen years, but why did it have to happen like this? Why now? It seemed too cruel to be real. I always took for granted that when the time came, I would be there with him, like we both deserved. I assumed I'd at least have a friend with me, and that I'd drown my sorrows in a bunch of martinis and a few laughs afterward at one of my favorite bars. But I wasn't getting that. I thought of all the people in the world having to say their final goodbyes to parents, siblings, and spouses on phone calls or over Zoom—if given the opportunity at all. There was such unimaginable loss being suffered at that time—far worse and more traumatic than what I was going through. But this was mine, and it fucking sucked.

• • • • •

In an effort to alleviate some of the horror of the situation and be somewhat ceremonial, I put on soft, classical music. I picked Mushi up and held him for the last time. I told him I would be okay, that it was okay to go, and that he wouldn't be alone. His eyes, which had been closed until now, suddenly opened a bit. I told him I loved him and he slowly blinked once, an indication (I've always chosen to believe) that he was saying it back.

I got a call from downstairs that Ben had arrived. My doorman, Joe, offered to come get the cat and bring him down for me.

"Be careful with him," I pleaded through sobs.

I wrapped Mushi in his blanket, put him in his carrier with one of his favorite toys, and placed it in the hallway outside my door (one of the most excruciating things I've ever had to do). I stood in the doorway, talking to him until I heard the elevator ring and saw Joe turn the corner. Careful to avoid contact, I said my final goodbye as I quickly closed the door. "Love you, sweet boy."

Fifteen minutes later, Ben called to let me know that he had successfully handed the carrier off to the nurse at the animal hospital. His girlfriend, Paige, had taken the drive with him, and he assured me that she sat in the back seat with him on her lap, talking to him the whole time. Another fifteen minutes after that, the vet called to let me know that Mushi had passed.

"He went very peacefully. We put him on his blanket with his toy. All the nurses came into the room for him, and he was surrounded with love."

My heart was broken and my quarantine quarters now seemed lonelier than ever. But that stormy afternoon, the dark clouds suddenly parted and the sun beamed brightly into my living room, casting a small rainbow on the photo of Mushi sitting on my desk. He was letting me know he'd made it safely. (He could've just texted.)

Two weeks later, an envelope arrived from an environmental non-profit organization. The card inside said that a grove of twenty trees had been planted in loving memory of Mushi Rainbow, courtesy of Carol Burnett. Well, you can't do better than that. I put the card on my windowsill next to Mushi's ashes, now safely housed in a hand-carved box I had engraved with the words SOMEWHERE ONLY WE KNOW . . .

• • • • •

Goodbye, my little Mush-man. Thank you for being my home for seventeen years. Thank you for growing up with me and always taking such good care of me. Thank you for being such a good listener (I know I'm long-winded at times), for making me laugh, and for being so understanding every time I locked you out of the bedroom to entertain a gentleman friend. I was just chasing a little tail. . . . You know how it is. Thank you for all the games of hide-and-seek (I never let you win on purpose . . . that was all you), and for getting so excited every time I came through the front door after a long weekend on the road. That meant a lot.

I'm sorry we didn't get to be together at the very end like I'd always planned, but you were not alone. You were surrounded with love. I'm writing about our story in this book and I hope that a few humans who've shared the same kind of love and loss will feel some comfort from it. I promise to keep you in my heart always and to take care of myself, like I know you'd want me to.

I got this.

19

Pink Glasses

I was fitted for my first pair of prescription glasses when I was twelve, and I hated them. I'm very nearsighted, so the lenses were as thick as Coke bottles and I had to wear them all the time. Trust me, it was a field day for school bullies, who already had plenty of material on me to work with. Finally getting contact lenses almost a decade later was one of the greatest things that ever happened for me, and a massive self-confidence boost. So it's ironic that everywhere I go these days, people are insistent—be it for selfies or photo shoots—that I put on my glasses.

The pink glasses I wear in many of my videos have become my signature. They even appear in my official logo. As I write this book, Live Nation is posting ads and hanging posters across the country promoting my "Pink Glasses Tour," which is scheduled to launch in fall of 2021. Just down the street from my apartment in Manhattan, a picture of me wearing the glasses appears on the marquee at the famous Beacon Theatre, alerting people to my upcoming concerts there. They started as nothing more than a cheap sight gag, but the Pink Glasses have since taken on a life of their own.

In one of my earliest political spoofs ahead of the 2016 election (I don't recall specifically which video it was), I thought it might be mildly amusing if, while acting like Anderson Cooper and pretending to conduct a serious interview, I suddenly put on a pair of ridiculous, pink, rhinestoned, cat-eye glasses I'd found buried in a bag of Halloween junk, the way journalists often do to show they mean business. I raised the glasses to my face as I spoke soberly and then stared through them with a deadpan expression at the interviewee (added later in editing) as he or she responded to my question. Just like that, a stare was born.

The glasses wound up being a big hit, and I noticed lots of people mentioning them in the comments. I started repeating the bit and before long, the Pink Glasses themselves had become a recurring character.

Through the years, I've gotten to hear from my audience just what the Pink Glasses symbolize to them. According to many, they are kind of like my queer superhero cape (my super-queero cape?). Whenever the unscrupulous subject of my satire starts acting shady, I put the glasses on and everyone knows it's time for a healthy dose of sass and show tunes.

People from all over the world have sent me photos of themselves and their families wearing their own Pink Glasses. Some put them on their children or pets for Halloween, some wear them to vote or march in protest, and some have even told me they've worn them to receive their chemotherapy treatments. I can't tell you how moved and honored I am by this.

They also happen to look super cute on everyone, and they're perfect for absolutely any occasion. I like to wear mine when I'm washing dishes, rewatching my favorite movie musicals, or blocking people on social media.

• • • • •

But practical utility and fashion sense aside, all this hoopla over my unconventional eyewear has got me thinking about what they've come to mean to me, and what I like to think they represent. The truth is, the Pink Glasses *are* magical. Yes . . . fundamentally, they're merely a cheap prop made of crappy plastic (now available for purchase on RandyRainbow.com!). But ever since I started wearing mine, they've taken me around the world and made my dreams come true. With my trusty Pink Glasses on, I've been able to say and do and be things I never imagined I'd have the chutzpah to say, do, or be. For me, they symbolize an exterior expression of my inner magic.

• • • • •

Some of the loveliest and most meaningful moments I've had over the last few years have been during the Q&A segments of my live shows. On multiple occasions, LGBTQ audience members from every age group have stood up and told me that I somehow helped or inspired them to come out and live their authentic lives. Parents of teens and young children have thanked me for being a role model to their kids by encouraging them to always be themselves. This kind of monumental praise was unexpected at first. Not only did I feel unworthy of it, I didn't really understand what they meant by it. I happily and humbly believe I might better understand now.

I've been acting flamboyantly, singing in girlish falsettos, and wearing lipstick in my videos for years. The reason I do these things, essentially, is that I'm giving a performance . . . and because I want to. (Also, let's face it, I happen to look goddamn adorable in drag.) Until people started pointing it out, though, it never occurred to me that this kind of uncurbed pageantry of mine could have any greater impact. More importantly, I came to realize that I was taking for granted whatever personal growth I must have attained somewhere along the way to have never thought twice about it. (Shout-out to the Billy Porters and Sean Hayeses of the world, who contributed so colossally to paving the way for artists like me. And shout-out to my own mother, who always created a safe space for me to be myself in those formative years.)

My hope is that the Pink Glasses serve as a badge of courage and the kind of moxie it takes to allow yourself to feel comfortable in your own skin. It might not always be easy, but it's the only way to be. Life's short . . . wear the fucking lipstick, gurl.

* * * * *

In November of 2020, I got an email from the legendary composer Alan Menken, which read:

Dear Randy—

As your main go-to composer, I wanted to give you a virtual hug for the great video masterpieces you've delighted us all with (well . . . 51% of us).

If you ever want to explore creating something from scratch, I'd love to discuss . . .

* * * * *

Phew! I thought he was gonna tell me he was suing me. You know I've ripped off *Beauty and the Beast* more times than Rudy Giuliani's ripped off the U.S. Constitution! Anyway, you can bet your Little Shop of Horrors I took him up on his offer. That's right, kiddos! I wrote a song with Alan fucking Menken, and it's called . . . "Pink Glasses"!

The song opens with a somewhat mythologized origin story of the Pink Glasses. It reveals that they once belonged to my grandmother, but because I loved them so much, she gifted them to me one rainy day in my childhood, describing all the special magic they hold.

(Nanny's main thrill in life was the occasional family trip we took to Disney World. She and I spent countless hours together enjoying the soundtracks to all the classic '90s Disney movies. Getting the opportunity to write lyrics about her to a song composed especially for me by Alan Menken was insanely emotional, and is almost too much joy to fit in my heart.)

In actuality, I do have a pair of my grandmother's glasses. When she passed, the family went to her condo to clear it out, and we each took a few of her personal belongings as mementos. One of the things I took was the pair of reading glasses that always sat on her bedroom nightstand, which in retrospect now seems somewhat prophetic. Above all, I like to think of the Pink Glasses as an emblem of truth through humor, and of the whimsical outlook on life I'm grateful to have inherited from my Nanny.

* * * * *

As far as I'm concerned, everyone has a pair of Pink Glasses tucked in their back pocket, whether they realize it or not. They're the key that unlocks all the joy, humor, creativity, and magic within you. They're a secret superpower that allows you to turn your biggest insecurities into your greatest assets. They're a sparkly, rose-colored lens through which you can see this crazy world however you want to see it. They're whatever gives you the courage to cut the shit, find your truth, and proudly put it out there on full display.

Consider this a personal prescription from your favorite fairy god-optometrist (that's me) to find your Pink Glasses, and wear them often.

20

Cleanup on Aisle '10

Okay, time to get serious for a few pages. . . .

* * * * *

People have been asking me for years: "So you must get tons of hate mail, huh?" My stock answer used to be, "Actually, you'd be surprised by how much hate mail I *don't* get," which was true. I mean, with the conversations about the topics I cover becoming as brutal as they have, who could get riled up over a few campy show tune parodies? (Right?)

I don't believe the tone of my content ever changed, but it seemed by 2020 that some of the reaction it was getting had. My intention remained, as always, to be humorous, but I began to question how seriously I was being taken by some. I noticed lots of people on one side retweeting my videos with vitriol and vengeance, lobbing them all over social media like "gotcha" missiles meant to target their rivals, who in turn were evaluating them like political ads, and me as though I were a pundit or politician myself. I was getting accused of being a neoliberal elitist. I don't even know what that means. I had to look it up while writing this paragraph and I still don't know what it means. "Why am I being scrutinized like this?" I kept asking myself. "I'm not the Lincoln Project . . . I'm just some schmuck with wigs!"

· · · · ·

The country was at an all-time low, which is saying a lot given the four years we had just been through. Not only was it an election year, it was *the* election year. And even that was upstaged by the devastating pandemic that was now sharing headlines with the racial reckoning that erupted in the wake of the horrific murder of George Floyd that May. It was a somber time to say the least, and people were generally and understandably not feeling lighthearted about much.

Since I'd been able to churn out content at an accelerated pace during a time when even late-night talk shows and *SNL* were on indefinite hiatus, I saw my numbers start to skyrocket. I was guesting (via Zoom, of course) on daytime TV shows like *The Talk.* A second Emmy nomination that July brought me even more press. My viewership and social media following were growing quickly, which meant—for better or worse—a lot more eyeballs on me. And, as it turned out, they weren't all heart-shaped eyeballs like on that horny smiley-face emoji. It was exciting to be recognized for all my hard work, but the spike in visibility was also unsettling. I could sense a storm was a-brewin'.

· · · · ·

My Andy Cuomo parody video was a particular bone of contention for many. Because my cat was dying when I released it, I guess I didn't quite process the intensity of the social media frenzy it had set off at the time. Many of Cuomo's harshest critics suddenly became mine.

"How the hell did I wind up in politics?" I asked myself, looking for the nearest exit. I only ever wanted to be Julie Andrews—not Nancy Pelosi! Naively, I never assumed people would view what I was doing as aggressive or offensive agenda-pushing. I suppose, in this day and age, that type of reaction just comes with the territory, but it's so antithetical to my intention. And this political scrutiny was not at all what I had in mind. Nevertheless, she persisted. . . .

That August, I released a song parody video called "Kamala" to the tune of "Camelot" (because, duh) in which I sang the praises of Joe Biden's newly selected running mate, Kamala Harris. Like the Cuomo video, "Kamala!" began trending almost immediately. Though the playful lyrics focused mostly on nonpartisan issues like the pronunciation of her name and the celebration of her historical achievements as a woman of color, many people seemed enraged by the video. Those who were not fans of the California senator or of the ticket in general were not happy with me.

This sure felt like a whole new ball game (not that I'd know what a ball game feels like). I guess it was hard for people—even ardent Trump supporters—to disagree with my musical chastising of him over the last four years, but it seemed any championing of other politicians, as benign or farcical as it may have been, was something I wasn't going to get away with so easily.

Just about eight hours after the "Kamala" video dropped, I started noticing an unusual influx of retweets on Twitter. They were not of my latest video as would normally be the case. These were retweets of tweets from ten years earlier—jokes I had tweeted (and long since forgotten), mostly in 2010, back when my comedy shtick was pretending to be Mel Gibson's totally clueless boyfriend. That whole series of YouTube sketches, in which I walked around having lovey-dovey phone conversations with Mel Gibson's vile, racist, anti-Semitic, and homophobic phone rants, was based on the absurd premise that I (a real-life gay Jew) was wacky and distasteful enough to date him.

They were all, in essence, cheap insult jokes—my own personal comedic spin on offensive tropes. They were racially insensitive and ambitiously poor in taste.

> How many (insert ethnic group) does it take to change a light bulb? Not making an offensive joke, just trying to post an ad on Craigslist.

> In honor of MLK Day, last night I had a dream: I dreamed Natalie Portman and I were eating Blizzards at Dairy Queen. You're welcome, Black People!

"Yeesh," I thought, "what asshole wrote these?" Then I realized, the asshole was me. My shitty first attempts at joke writing were cringeworthy, to say the least. And viewed through the cold, harsh prism of present day, nothing short of mortifying. Dozens of profiles were now spreading them around with captions like "This you, @RandyRainbow?" and "Care to explain, RR?"

At first glance they were shocking, even to me. But I was quickly able to contextualize them, at least for myself. I could totally see what I was trying to do back then, and no, it was not audition to become a member of the Proud Boys. I was in character, playing a dimwit . . . a "Karen," and trying my darnedest to be edgy and provocative. I was testing material on a very small and contained Twitter audience, all of whom I knew were in on the joke. I wasn't mocking any one race, I was mocking racists and racism itself. I wasn't saying what I actually believe—that racism is wrong. I was saying the opposite and embracing racism as the boyfriend of someone despicable. And, that was the joke. I was emulating a style of comedy that was, for better or worse, prevalent at the time. *The Sarah Silverman Program* was on basic cable back then, and comedian Lisa Lampanelli was headlining all over the globe with far edgier material than what I was tweeting.

I'd say this style of roast humor began to die about twelve minutes after I started experimenting with it. The idea of "offend everyone ironically to prove you love everyone actually" was getting lost in translation, and many liberal-minded comedians who'd been tightly clutching onto the philosophy that "No, it's okay . . . I'm not racist so I can say racist stuff in jest" were getting wise to the fact that maybe it wasn't true after all. Like many of my more contemporary comedy idols, I quickly took the note. What's more, I eventually evolved my satire to target actual bigoted jerks, rather than embodying one myself.

It never occurred to me to delete these old tweets, which had just been collecting dust for ten or more years. I never felt I had anything to hide. They were just jokes. I'd been working in gay nightclubs in New York City around that time. These were the kind of low-brow antics we'd get laughs with onstage, from the most eclectic and multicultural crowds. Sure, my style had changed since then, and I always figured there was probably material in my archives that wouldn't pass muster today. Hell, there are episodes of sitcoms from just two years ago being pulled from the airwaves because they're no longer deemed appropriate by today's standards. In this rapidly shifting culture, that's the name of the game. If the expiration dates on these jokes weren't enough clarification to anyone who happened upon them, I felt confident enough that I had firmly established my social media platform as my comedy stage. What existed online was not my personal diary. I mean, all of the recognition and press I was getting was based on the conceit that I burst into Broadway production numbers at presidential press conferences, and had nonsensical conversations with politicians who weren't actually in the room. None of this shit is real, folks.

I was an unknown twenty-something back then with virtually no platform. But these long-expired jokes being retweeted from my now-verified profile with a significantly larger following and "public figure" status in 2020 read more like hate speech than stale comedy.

· · · · ·

In a frenzy, I was now deleting each one as it popped up. In retrospect I realized this was the equivalent of hiding the murder weapon. It didn't matter anyway. By now, they had all been screenshotted and were spreading like wildfire. Collages were compiled with samples of my asinine, "Karen"-esque wisecracks and every time I used the pejorative for "transgender" (a word that had been considered acceptable slang a decade earlier by many in the gay community and even mainstream entertainment until GLAAD taught us better). I was being branded racist and transphobic. Even self-deprecating jokes I'd made about my own Jewishness and homosexuality were stripped of their personal context and marked as anti-Semitic and homophobic.

Yahoo News and Variety.com had begun posting articles with headlines like CANCEL CULTURE COMES FOR RANDY RAINBOW. Popular LGBTQ sites quickly joined the chorus in more dramatic fashion. One posted an article titled RANDY RAINBOW GOES INTO HIDING AFTER DOZENS OF OLD RACIST AND TRANSPHOBIC TWEETS RESURFACE. (Okay, I hadn't tweeted in about a day and a half, but, "goes into hiding"? It was the middle of a pandemic. I was sitting on my couch, where I'd been for the last five months. Calm down, girl.) Another posted a long, detailed breakdown of every ethnic group, religion, and gender I'd "targeted."

An important distinction being omitted from many of these articles was the fact that I was a comedian and that the tweets were jokes (admittedly lousy and offensive ones). They were being presented as if they were genuine sentiments, or drunken rants caught on tape. What was now being called into question was my personal character—not my persona or the comedic character I was playing. These jokes deserved to be criticized, and the discussion of my personal artistic evolution (or the evolution of comedy in general) is one in which I'm happy to participate. I also accept full accountability for past mistakes, in my work and otherwise. But criticism of my sloppy efforts as a young comedian was being conflated with conjecture about my basic decency as an actual human. The critics were ignoring the satire—my Scotch Tape on the "balloon"—and suddenly I was nothing but a prick.

Even in the height of the anxiety, regret, and embarrassment I was feeling, I also couldn't help but step back to marvel at the ultimate irony of the situation, and how telling it was about the place at which we'd arrived culturally. The gimmick that essentially launched this career of mine was the bizarre pretense that I was Mel Gibson's boyfriend. That sketch established my comedy persona and first audience. Now on Mel's and my tenth anniversary, that old comedy was having an unauthorized revival. And stripped of all the context and nuance of my first viral video, "Randy Rainbow Is Dating Mel Gibson," Randy Rainbow was now actually accused of *being* Mel Gibson.

By the next day, my friend and publicist, Victoria, was receiving requests from various outlets asking for an official statement.

"I have to post a video explaining all this," I told her, nervously pacing through my apartment.

"Don't post anything. You need to address this, but I want you to do it the right way."

The Advocate magazine had reached out offering to interview me. Victoria arranged for me to talk with them the next morning.

I knew there were plenty of people completely uninterested in hearing the well-organized defense I was so eager to present. Bloggers and furloughed gossip columnists were more than happy to run with the clickbait, and those who didn't like me to begin with were relishing the schadenfreude of seeing the guy who'd stuck it to Trump for all his batshit, bigoted tweets over the years now getting the pie right back in his own face. I didn't care much about that. What was really upsetting to me was the thought that any fans of mine unfamiliar with my comedy origin story or people who were feeling the weight of our harsh world couldn't see the jokes for what they were during 2020, a time of hatred, pandemic, and the rise of racial persecution. All they were seeing were these awful headlines. I wanted to explain myself to them. I wanted to apologize.

My panic turned to heartbreak. I felt ashamed, as though I'd let everyone down. I felt as though I'd let myself down. I was proud of how far I'd come and of all the work I'd done over the past four years . . . over the past ten years. I was using my platform for good, and in my own campy way, taking a stand for truth and equality (things that were genuinely important to me). There was so much racial tension in the world and so much injustice coming to light. It was the summer of Black Lives Matter. I wanted to continue to be a positive voice. I was nearing forty and finally felt like I'd grown up. This hacky, outdated shtick—this blip from my twenties—was not at all how I wanted to be represented, creatively or any other way.

I got a text from Tituss, who had apparently just read the news on me, and was obviously reading my mind, too.

You did nothing wrong. People are just bored. This will blow over. I'm here if you need me.

Immediately after he sent the text, he went on his own Twitter account and posted a string of rebuttals in my defense. We hadn't spoken in over a year, but my big brother was right there when I needed him.

I barely slept that night. The next morning, as I lay in bed waiting for the hours to pass until my interview, I asked Nanny to help guide me through this gracefully, with love, clarity, and humor.

"Give me a sign you're with me, Nan."

I thought of her favorite expression: "This too shall pass." A pretty run-of-the-mill adage, I know, but in our family, very Nanny-specific. My uncle Andy even has it tattooed on his arm in her memory. In this moment, it was exactly what I needed to hear.

Finally, the co–editor in chief of *The Advocate* called.

"Hi, Randy. How are you doing?"

"You know what, David? I've been better."

"I hear you. Well, we're big fans here at *The Advocate*. We know your heart, and we're happy to give you an opportunity to speak about this."

"I really appreciate it. It's been a rough few days."

"I'm sure it has," he said, "but this too shall pass."

At this point, I burst into tears like a lunatic. I'm sure the poor guy must have thought I'd flipped my lid.

"Sorry to be so emotional, David," I said through my sniffles. "My grandmother just walked into the room."

· · · · ·

The Advocate piece posted later that afternoon, and the response was generally quite positive. Lots of strangers kindly reached out to accept my apology, and many of my friends in the comedy world seemed proud of the logical analysis I also gave about my professional process in the interview.

I was still getting dragged on Twitter, though. And I mean dragged . . . like, by actual drag queens. It seemed remarkable to me how many who lined up to snatch my morality wig had apparently never heard of insult comedy.

"How come it took you ten years to address this?" one tweeted at me, as though the FBI had just uncovered my involvement in the Madoff investment scandal of 2008.

The truth, however, was that I had addressed it. As a topical and sometimes polarizing comedian, I'm asked frequently about the state of comedy, where the lines are, and what's on the table or off-limits. I had spoken candidly in multiple interviews throughout the years about my own development, and language or content I once believed was acceptable now being untouchable.

I had never heard from any of these Good Samaritans in all the years I'd been using my comedy for good, hosting benefits and donating time and resources to charitable organizations. They had never been interested in acknowledging the positive work I'd done. But now, the moment they saw a little blood in the water, you can damn well bet they swam right over to take a bite. A lot of friends in the industry started contacting me.

"Move on," the great Carol Burnett told me on a call later that day. "There are so many of us who love you. There'll always be critics. Don't do them the honor of thinking about this another minute."

One of my friends, the insanely hilarious and brutally no-bullshit comedian Judy Gold, had just written a book on the topic of free speech in comedy called *Yes I Can Say That: When They Come for the Comedians, We Are All in Trouble*. I called her right up.

"Judy . . . I'm in trouble."

As always, I knew I could count on Judy for her calm, levelheaded, and completely unbiased take—

"Fuck this! Fuck this fucking bullshit! This is so fucked! We literally have a president throwing kids in fucking cages and trying to kill us all with fucking bleach during a pandemic and these fuckers have the nerve to come for you, of all people, about fucking jokes?!? Fuck!!!"

By the time I hung up with Judy, my sadness started turning to anger. "Yeah, fuck this," I thought. "I'm a good person! I'm not a politician . . . I'm a comedian!" (Not that there's much of a difference these days.) These tweets weren't skeletons in my closet . . . they were crappy jokes in my shoebox! They were not oaths I took in blood . . . they were scripted one-liners. How could anyone claim to make a legitimate judgment about my character when what they were actually judging was the character of the *character* I was playing?! It was like if the feds had dug up an old VHS tape of me playing Sky Masterson in my high school production of *Guys and Dolls* and said, "Mr. Rainbow, we've found this footage of you running an illegal underground crap game in the '90s. Please come with us." That was just an embarrassing old performance, and so was this.

I started to find all this pearl-clutching incredibly disingenuous and hypocritical.

One of the LGBTQ sites now vilifying me had been following me since my humble beginnings in 2010. They'd had a front-row seat to every word of every joke I ever tweeted in those days, yet nary a plucked eyebrow was raised at the time. There was no concern in all the years since, when the time came to profit from posting my videos, that they were promoting the work of a deranged bigot. Now that I was in some hot water, they were turning me in faster than a mob of pro-life whistleblowers in Texas.

I remembered a popular story that same site had posted back in 2014, praising the great Bianca Del Rio (my brilliant friend Roy Haylock, who I adore and worship) for handling a heckler who criticized her use of racial humor. It praised "the fast-talking Southern charmer" for "shutting that shit down" and "handing her critic's ass right back to him." Another outlet added that the offended audience member "obviously did not realize that comedians and drag queens say offensive things all the time without reprimands from the PC police."

The gay press on this particular incident from 2014 looked like a full-out "YAS KWEEN" for free speech in the name of comedy. It seemed like a double standard that my similarly styled jokes from even further back should now be retroactively judged so unforgivingly. I guess I shoulda been a drag queen like my mother said.

And don't get me wrong. The sight of my flippant use of the "t-word" (the offensive and unacceptable slang for "transgender") from 2010 made me wanna vomit in 2020. But let's be real. There were articles in freakin' *Oprah Magazine* from that time celebrating an LGBTQ star of the prime-time hit show *Project Runway* for his positive and loving connotation of the word. Catchphrases with it were being sold on mugs and T-shirts. Times change! People learn!

• • • • •

All my indignation had melted away by that night, and underneath, just waiting to make an entrance, were my old pals anxiety and depression. It had officially been determined by now that this archeological Twitter dig had in fact been meticulously planned and executed by a certain political group hoping to smear me (who am I . . . Julian Assange?). But none of that mattered to me anymore. It felt like my narrative and my truth had been hijacked. I felt I'd lost all control, and quickly spiraled to an extreme level of sadness I hadn't experienced in a long time, if ever. Up till now, amid the unrelenting horror of the world crashing in around me—the pandemic, the isolation, the cat, the fucking election— the one thing holding me together was the outlet for my creative work. Not only was it bringing some solace to others, it was a joyful distraction for me. Now all that was on hold indefinitely, and seemingly in jeopardy.

I was also now cut off from my supply of the dangerous and highly addictive drug my other pal, social media, had been dealing me so regularly: the approval of strangers. The steady stream of dopamine I was getting from all the positive reinforcement and good press had, to some extent, been numbing all the bad stuff. Suddenly I couldn't even rely on that for a quick fix. My magic mirror (my iPhone) was no longer telling me I was the fairest one of all. In fact, it was telling me I was a real asshole. I think for a while I started to believe it. For the first time in a long time, I truly felt alone with myself. And now even I didn't wanna play with me.

• • • • •

I hadn't slept in days and had barely eaten (usually the stage in my depression cycle before the one where I eat literally everything). Calls and texts kept coming in from friends. It's amazing how much a little Twitter controversy can reveal about your inner circle. As it turned out, though, some of the most meaningful calls and advice were coming from the outside.

A couple of days after the *Advocate* article posted, I got a DM from Leslie Odom, Jr. It was his phone number and then, **You're doing a great job. You can beat this with your creativity and open heart. Call me so I can give you some love.**

We had only met once before, when I was interviewing him on the red carpet of an after-party for the off-Broadway opening of *Hamilton* at The Public Theater in 2015. To my thrill, he was effusive about my web series, and it had been a real mutual admiration society ever since. (Fun Fact: Between the two of us, we have a total of one Tony Award.)

I called him right away, and we talked for an hour. He was so nurturing and full of wisdom. I kept thinking about what a great dad he must be. I wished he were mine.

"Put me on the list of people you run stuff by," he insisted. "I always wanna be on that list."

His intense generosity rendered me speechless—for a few seconds, anyway. Then, in my sleep-deprived stupor, I started rattling off the list of defenses I'd been pacing around with in my head for days.

"Leslie, they don't understand . . . I was just trying to do jokes. . . . It was a different time . . . I was trying to be edgy and Sarah Silverman made a movie once and I was dating Mel Gibson and—"

"Randy," he cut me off, "I totally get it . . . and nobody gives a shit. We're in a moment right now. This will always be a part of your history. There will always be someone bringing it up to you, but you can own it. I mean, you were that little boy on the playground who got bullied for being different . . ."

(Hey, wait a minute . . . how did he know my life?)

"And now look at you. You put on those damn pink glasses and that lipstick and wear it all like a badge of honor. You made it yours. Turn this into humor, too. Express it through your comedy. Wear it like you wear your Pink Glasses and we'll all love you that much more for it."

(Damn, he's good.)

"And don't shy away from any opportunity to teach younger kids. Tell them why you thought it was okay to do those kinds of jokes back then."

My new father, Leslie Odom, Jr., was right. I was so busy defending the little kid in me from faceless Twitter trolls, I hadn't considered the teachable moment in all this—for myself or anyone else. I hadn't considered many things. Why *did* I think it was okay, as green as I was back then, to fast-track myself to that ambitiously risqué brand of satire? Aside from looking for laughs and attention, I think because I myself am a proud member of two marginalized groups, I was acting on a sense of entitlement that made me feel I had a free pass. I've also heard some of the comedians I was mimicking in those days hypothesize in retrospect that because we finally saw a man of color in the White House, some comics (naively assuming many of our country's race problems were now in the rear view) figured it was culturally safe enough to push those limits.

I personally felt fairly limitless in my twenties, and was allowing myself to experiment with a degree of reckless abandon. I was unclear about where certain lines should be drawn, if and when a line should be crossed at all, and sometimes unaware I was even going near a line.

One of my earliest videos, back before Mel Gibson in 2010, featured a scene where I (in character) had become so obsessed with Oprah (that part was based on real life) that by the end, I briefly morphed into her. To accomplish the effect, I wore drag that included foundation a good seven shades deeper than my own complexion. When I first went on tour years later, people at my meet and greets started asking me to remove the video from my archives because they rightfully found it offensive, but my clueless self way back then was surprised by the backlash.

"Oh, that old thing??? No, that's not what that is," I'd say, brushing them off high-handedly. I was well versed in the good, bad, and ugly history of show business. To me, blackface was the distinctive and categorically racist style of performance depicted in pictures of minstrel shows from the early nineteenth century and by Al Jolson in *The Jazz Singer*. This was by no means that, I thought, "And how dare they offend *me* by even insinuating that my humorous intentions would be so malicious!?" I was ignorant of the fact that even an homage using CoverGirl to play a celebrity in sketch comedy was, of course, viewed as an offensive callback to many. As my fan base grew, calls to remove the old video became louder and more frequent. I finally realized my mistake and took it down a few months after the negative responses started coming, but it took a number of people to teach me the lesson I needed to learn. I was so hell-bent on defending my comedic intentions, I callously forgot to consider the notion that maybe sometimes even my precious intentions don't fucking matter.

The social media age, with all its horrors, has given us a window into other people's life experiences and perspectives. It's been enlightening—certainly for me—and given us insights that of course have changed us for the better.

* * * * *

I wanted to honor Leslie's advice and handle this, at least in some way, with humor. Now that Randy the person had addressed his old jokes, it was time for Randy the character to do the same. In the intro for my next song parody release, I faked an interview with Trump following *his* most recent Twitter controversy (who can remember which one?), taking time to acknowledge that the two of us were finally sharing some common ground.

"Listen, I get it," I assured him. "I was once an aspiring comedian just like you! I posted offensive things for shock value. The difference is, I was doing it satirically—using irony and exaggeration to point out absurdity. . . . But I quickly changed my act when I realized there were *actually* awful things *actually* being said and done by *actually* awful people . . . just like you!"

It was more a light scar than a badge of honor, but it felt good to finally own it. I never expect it to disappear. There will always be people with screenshots of those old jokes eager to embarrass or make an example of me. Those same people will likely have screenshots of jokes I'm tweeting now that in ten years will be considered complete blasphemy. The lines of acceptability are rapidly shifting. Old comedy in the age of social media is a bit like Pennywise the Clown from Stephen King's *It*. It's messy and abstract and it comes back every decade or so to torment you. There's nothing (short of pelting chunks of silver at its skull with my slingshot) I can do about it. But I'll always take every opportunity—like this one right here—to apologize to anyone I genuinely offended. There's no fun in offending others, and it's never my intention.

As for the armchair activists, opportunistic media outlets, bullies, and bots who came out of the woodwork to take a bite when they saw some blood, whose condemnations in the name of "tolerance" were so passive-aggressively laced with anti-Semitism and homophobia, who threatened my safety or branded me a bigot for singing the praises of a candidate at whom they were simultaneously hurling actual racism and misogny . . . well, I guess I'll take Carol's advice and not do them the honor.

To those whose passion sincerely lies in effecting positive change, who have a real stake in dispelling racism and intolerance in all their forms, and whose important work led to the cultural upheaval we saw in 2020 and beyond, please know how much I respect and appreciate you. You've taught many, including myself, the importance of accountability and that small horrors often maintain pathways for bigger ones. Just as I believe comedy should not be evaluated as harshly as dangerous political rhetoric or real hate speech, I also believe that self-serving virtue-signaling and faceless Twitter trolling should never be conflated with true political activism.

● ● ● ● ●

I've written and rewritten the end of this chapter a dozen times, trying to wrap it up neatly—trying to decide exactly where I stand and what my intention is now. To be perfectly honest, I'm not entirely sure. It's just not that nice and neat. I hope in some way this serves as a cautionary tale about the lasting effects of social media and the risks of opinions, art, and even bold fashion choices being examined well beyond their expiration dates. I hope someone as stubborn as I am gleans something from the lessons I've learned about letting your defenses down occasionally and being truly as open-minded as you like to think you are.

That said, I would also never want to discourage risk-taking in comedy. With risk comes the potential for epic failure, as I've just illustrated. But when it works, there's nothing else like it. Many people are quick to write off comedians who joke about serious topics as uncaring or disrespectful, when in fact the comedian is giving those jokes and topics his/her/their full professional attention.

Over the years, I've heard from people in the midst of the worst circumstances and tragedies who have graciously thanked me for making them laugh and bringing some light to their unimaginable traumas. I'm so honored to be able to give them a brief "vacation" (as insignificant as it may seem) from such unthinkable realities. The only way I've been able to do that has been by taking risks.

And at the risk of sounding completely self-interested, I really hope we can return to some semblance of a culture in which context and nuance in comedy and art get the consideration they so deserve and rely upon. I know it's confusing because we all tweet in the same Helvetica Neue (or whatever-the-hell font Twitter is using these days), but the politician's statements and viewpoints—past, present, or future—are not the same as the comedian's jokes. They should not be judged the same.

I think a lot about an observation I recently heard by Sam Harris (the philosopher and neuroscientist, not the Broadway singer who I massively crushed on in the eleventh grade):

You could hire someone who has been convicted of murder . . . served their time . . . and you are now part of their redemption story. And the same people who would try to destroy you for having hired someone who's trailing some bad tweets would celebrate you for hiring someone who killed a family and has been brought back into some sphere of redemption and forgiven.

Look, I don't have all the answers. That's why I quote neuroscientists who are much smarter than me (sorry . . . "much smarter than I"). I'm sure I'm wrong about a lot of shit, but at the end of the day, all I can do is my best. Lipstick aside, I am not flawless. I've made many mistakes—privately and publicly—and though I continue to learn and grow every day, I'm sure there's plenty more where those came from. Hell, I've probably just written fifteen things in this chapter alone that will get me canceled by next Thursday. Don't be surprised if this very important and heartfelt section of the book is replaced by my aunt Rita's tuna casserole recipe in the paperback edition.

21

Patti Fucking LuPone

"Patti LuPone is looking for you."

"Oh, fuck," I replied on a call with my agent in early September of 2020. "What did I do?"

For years, I'd been dreaming of/dreading the day when my legendary muse would call. I had spent years parodying some of the most intimate and revealing accounts of her personal and professional life from her memoir in one of my earliest web series for the theatre site BroadwayWorld.com. It wasn't always easy making comedy out of theatre headlines, which was my job back then, so on slow news weeks I had to get extra creative. I was listening to the audiobook version of *Patti LuPone: A Memoir* (if you haven't, you must), which is read by Patti LuPone herself, and came up with the idea of lip-syncing portions of it. I'd wear lipstick and wigs and campily reenact the most dramatic passages. (This, of course, was long before everyone was lip-syncing literally everything on TikTok. I'm not saying my early work was completely revolutionary, but hey, check the receipts.) The segment became the most popular of the series, and some of my finest lip-syncing work to date, if I do say.

I never heard from Patti about it back in those days or in all the years since. It was clearly intended as a loving, if not oddly obsessive tribute by an adoring, if not slightly deranged fan. I also knew from actually reading her memoir that she had a healthy sense of humor. Still, you never know. I always feared that when I finally did get a call from her, it would involve litigation.

"She wants to collaborate with you," my agent said.

Triple pirouette, ball change, fan kick, aaaaand death drop!

· · · · ·

I'd actually been seeing quite a bit of Patti LuPone (virtually, that is) in the early days of the pandemic. The first time was on Seth Rudetsky's interview series *Stars in the House*. I was his guest for the hour and just as he got me to talk about my old lip-sync videos, he surprised me by bringing Patti LuPone onto the livestream, direct from her basement in Connecticut. Naturally I lost my shit. Thankfully, she was almost as excited to meet me. More importantly, there were no lawyers present.

The second time was for Stephen Sondheim's 90th Birthday Celebration. Since a live event was impossible that year, Broadway.com planned a prerecorded web concert featuring some of the biggest stars of stage and screen. Raúl Esparza, who was coproducing the show, called me up and asked if I'd do a song. He suggested I gender-bend *something* from *Sweeney Todd* or *Into the Woods*. Needless to say, he didn't have to twist my arm. Later that week, I filmed a version of the Mrs. Lovett song "By the Sea" from *Sweeney*.

On the night of the concert, all participants were invited to a Zoom room for a preshow "cast party." There on my computer screen were Patti, Mandy Patinkin, Bernadette Peters, Donna Murphy, Audra McDonald,

Jake Gyllenhaal, Neil Patrick Harris, Meryl Streep, and, of course, Sondheim himself, to list only a few. I couldn't believe it . . . I was the biggest name in the room.

The following Sunday, *The New York Times* reviewed the concert and included a photo of myself and a few of the other performers on the cover of their Arts & Leisure section. I was still too scared to leave my apartment, so I called down to my doorman and asked if I could pay him to run to the 7-Eleven next door and grab me a copy. "Sending my doorman to fetch the paper so I can see my review in a story about Sondheim's birthday concert . . . ," I thought to myself. "My transformation into Elaine Stritch is finally complete." *The Times* later did a podcast discussing the concert. While mentioning my performance, the host noted the irony of how, in the midst of a pandemic, all these megastars were suddenly "on Randy Rainbow's turf," forced to film themselves singing show tunes in their own living rooms. (Not as easy as it looks, huh, Meryl??)

Virtual or not, it was a real thrill to be included that night. I of course would have preferred the real thing. It had always been a dream of mine to be part of one of Sondheim's illustrious birthday concerts. Just my luck, I finally get invited and it's via green screen. Still, it was a dream-come-true-ish. It was actually on the 1993 PBS broadcast of *Sondheim: A Celebration at Carnegie Hall* that I was first introduced to Patti LuPone. As I've since told Patti, her rendition of "Being Alive" from that concert is basically what made me gay.

Okay, fine, I'm being dramatic. It didn't *actually* make me gay . . . that's just obnoxiously stereotyped hyperbole for the sake of a cheap laugh. It definitely made me a bottom, though.

• • • • •

I found out why Patti wanted to meet with me a couple of days after the call came from my agent. Mary Trump's book *Too Much and Never*

Enough about her uncle had just been released and was starting to get major press. At some point, I tweeted, "If Patti LuPone narrates the audio version of Mary Trump's book, I will lip-sync the entire thing." Apparently, Patti LuPone was intrigued.

"So, doll, how can we make this happen?" she asked on a video conference call a few days later.

I was so excited and also a little trepidatious. Truth is, my tweet was kind of just a joke. I wasn't sure that gimmick would actually work. I mean, sure, in theory, it would have been amazing. But I didn't know what type of clearances would be required, or if the book would still be in the headlines by the time we got it all sorted out. Because of the high-profile nature of the subject matter, this had viral potential and needed to be handled properly. Not to mention the insane buzz a long-awaited collaboration between two legendary Broadway icons like me and Patti LuPone would surely generate! (Fun Fact: Between the two of us, we have a total of two Best Leading Actress in a Musical Tony Awards.)

I got a sudden jolt of confidence and presented her with a plan B.

"I'm not sure that idea will work, Patti, but I do have another suggestion—and feel free to tell me to go fuck myself—but I was wondering if perhaps, under any circumstances, you would possibly consider maybe singing a duet with me?" I barely got the question out before she responded . . .

"In a fucking heartbeat!"

We decided I'd come up with a few parody ideas with lyric samples for her to choose from and we'd take it from there. Before we hung up, she told me she was excited to sing with me.

"I watch your videos and study your vocal technique," she said. Why was I not recording this call??? I picked my jaw up off the floor and then let her in on my secret.

"I hate to tell you, Patti, but my only technique is trying to sing like Patti LuPone."

· · · · ·

I knew from Patti's fabulously profanity-laced viral interviews about Trump over the years that she wasn't shy about her politics, so I went there in my writing samples. We quickly settled on a parody called "If Donald Got Fired" to the tune of "If Momma Was Married" from *Gypsy* to commemorate the first presidential debate of 2020. We recorded the track remotely from our respective homes, and planned for Patti to come to my apartment (WHAT?!?!) to film her part of the video.

Naturally, I was dizzy with excitement, but also nervous as hell. Not because Patti LuPone was coming over, but because, due to the pandemic, I hadn't had visitors in over six months. I had always been a germaphobe (apologies to all germs and their allies), but until all this went down, aside from my tour band constantly mocking my obsession with Bath & Body Works hand sanitizer, I didn't realize just how much. Adding to my anxiety, Patti's assistant emailed asking if there'd be a place for Patti to have her hair and makeup done when she arrived for the shoot.

"I'll handle it," said my friend, publicist, and therapist, Victoria. "I'll just tell them you're being extremely cautious about the number of guests you're allowing and that she'll have to come camera-ready. I'm sure everyone will understand."

· · · · ·

One week later, Patti LuPone arrived at my apartment with a full hair and makeup team.

"Doll, is it okay if they just come in to touch me up?" Patti asked, making her entrance through my front door. "Everyone's masked!"

"Sure," I said casually, hiding any hint of terror in my voice. "Screw it," I decided. I mean, I would be a disgrace to my community if I weren't willing to put my life on the line so that Patti LuPone could get her hair and makeup done in my living room.

"Great place!" she said, making her way to the center of the apartment and almost immediately spotting the copy of her memoir on my coffee table. "Hardcover edition! Nice!" (This was not strategic product placement, by the way, that's just where it lives.)

As she primped in the mirror hanging above my bar cabinet, we talked about the state of the world and of the theatre. She told me how emotional it was for her to leave the Bernard B. Jacobs Theatre that past March, having just opened the revival of *Company*. She said it crossed her mind as she packed up her dressing room and said her goodbyes to her castmates, not knowing what the future held, that she was possibly saying her final goodbye to Broadway, too. She started to cry as she spoke, at which point I got emotional.

"Not on my watch, Patti LuPone!" I said, lightening the mood. (I'm happy to report, at the time of this writing, the revival of *Company* with Patti LuPone is set to return to Broadway in fall of 2021. I've been invited to opening night.)

• • • • •

We headed into my studio to shoot. I fed Patti her dialogue cues from off camera. When it was time to film the song portion, she did her first take, mouthing her lyrics to the track. I couldn't believe it. After all the years I spent lip-syncing to Patti LuPone in front of that camera, there was Patti LuPone standing in front of the very same camera, lip-syncing . . . to Patti LuPone!

After one run-through, she said, "I think it'll look more realistic if I actually sing."

"Uh, no arguments here, Patti," I assured her. There she stood in the tiny converted bedroom decorated with multiple Broadway posters boasting her name and face, in front of my green screen, belting multiple takes full-out until we got what we needed. (I may have lied a little and requested a few more than we actually needed.) I will never recover.

•　•　•　•　•

A few days after the video was released, I got a text from PATTI FUCKING LUPONE (that is how she's listed in my phone):

Hey, Doll. I'm on the Upper West Side next week. Dinner?

We met a week later to dine alfresco at an Italian restaurant on Columbus Avenue. It was my first time at a restaurant in almost seven months. She was so warm and hilarious. We became fast friends. We talked Broadway, politics, our hometown on Long Island, took a few selfies, got tipsy on white wine (fine, I got a little drunk), and had a lot of laughs. A girl at the table next to ours recognized us both and asked for a photo.

"Look at us," I said to Patti. "We're a real sister act now!"

•　•　•　•　•

I floated home on a cloud. I thought about my friend Vanessa and how once when we were listening to the original cast recording of *Evita* as teenagers, she leapt up on the couch, Tom Cruise circa Katie Holmes style, and announced, "One day I'm gonna be friends with Patti LuPone!"

"Bullshit," I assured her. "We're just two stupid kids in South Florida. She'll never know who we are." I thought about how a few years later I was sitting behind the reception desk answering phones for a Broadway producer, and how fast my heart raced when she came in one afternoon to meet with her company manager. I thought about how a quirky lip-syncing shtick I randomly concocted a few years after that—reenacting her memoir on the internet—had oddly played a substantial role in my artistic trajectory, and how in some fateful, cosmic way, it all inexplicably led me to this night. As Oprah would say, it was a full "holy shit, I just had dinner with Patti fucking LuPone" moment.

I'm writing about it now in my own memoir to let anyone who reads this know that those crazy, fantastical, impossible, ain't-no-way, "bullshit, that could never happen" dreams that you dare—and sometimes don't even dare—to dream are not necessarily as impossible as you might think. (I'm also writing about it to make my friend Vanessa extremely jealous.)

Speaking of my memoir . . . I just thought of something else. . . . Wouldn't it be amazing if, just to fuck with me, Patti LuPone started a web series where she lip-synced the audio version of this book???

Hey, you never know. . . .

22

Ladies and Gentlemen, My Mother...

We're live in five, four, three . . .

Welcome back, everybody! We have a very exciting chapter planned for you tonight. We have a marvelous special guest about to join us, but before we welcome her to the book, let's take a look at the text message she sent me this morning to give you a glimpse of just one of the reasons why I am a neurotic, anxiety-ridden mess!

6:57am

> I just emailed you a NY Times article about an emergency security update they want us to do.

> It says update your Macs too. All Apple products.

Just occurred to me. When you go on tour, everyone traveling with you needs to be Covid tested on a schedule.

You 2. Rapid test!

Randy

Mom, could u wait till after 7am to trigger my every anxiety?

Sorry

7:03am

Did you update your phone yet?

Ladies and gentlemen, making her memoir debut, the woman responsible for my love of the arts, my solid moral compass, my dry sense of humor, and some of my most adorable facial expressions . . . my mom, Gwen!

(APPLAUSE)

Randy: Mom, thanks so much for being here!

Mom: How long is this gonna take? I have my book club in an hour.

Randy: Hey, speaking of books, can you believe I wrote one? You're actually in it right now!

Mom: I only saw you read one book as a child, and that was Stephen King's *It*. So I was expecting this to be a lot scarier.

(RIMSHOT)

Randy: So, give everyone the inside scoop: What was I like as a child? Was I as delightful as I remember?

Mom: Eh . . .

Randy: Mom!

Mom: No, you were very delightful. You had lots of friends, lots of playdates, and we had great adventures together. No tantrums, no trouble in school. Just a model child.

Randy: You used to put me to sleep with cast albums from musicals like *Oklahoma* and *The Music Man*. Was it a concerted effort to introduce me to musical theatre?

Mom: It was just the music I loved. In all fairness, I also put you to bed with Frank Zappa's *We're Only in It for the Money*, so maybe you didn't have much of an ear. I'm grateful you went toward musical theatre. It could have gone a very different way.

Randy: I don't know . . . wasn't Frank Zappa known for his satire of American culture?

Mom: Oh yeah, that's true! So, yes, I take full credit for all of your success.

Randy: Calm down. Were you aware of how gay you were making me/secretly hoping for it?

Mom: As much as I'd like to take credit for that, I really think you came that way. But I certainly didn't discourage it. What mother of one child doesn't want her little boy to also like wearing tights and ballet shoes? The perfect package.

Randy: Jokes aside, when did you first start to notice I was different from other little boys? Was it the pajama pants I wore on my head? The Ruby Slippers?

Mom: I guess the pajama pants were a big clue. Your little friend had long pigtails and you wanted them too. So you figured out the pajama pants—footed pj's, I might add—and then I had to make sure that the bows were exactly right on each "pigtail" and you would flip them in the air. My friends remember that flip to this day.

Randy: Yaaaaaaas!

Mom: We all had your number, Randy. Never saw you pick up a toy car and vroom it across the floor, either. But the real answer is that I never thought of you as being different from other little boys, I just thought you were you. Plus you had this really ridiculous name to live up to. What else could we expect, with that name?

Randy: Yeah, you must have known how miserable my childhood was gonna be with this name. Like, why did you hate me so much?

Mom: Well, we gave you a really boring middle name, just in case you became a lawyer and wanted to drop the "Rainbow."

Randy: Don't you dare reveal my middle name to all of America right now—

Mom: Stewart! It's not that bad. It was good enough for Jon Stewart.

Randy: True. I never really had to come out to you. You kind of did it for me. Do you remember it like that? And were you at all surprised when I confirmed?

Mom: I knew you were gay from a very early age . . . your early age, not mine. The Mary Poppins costumes, the sequins, the My Little Pony collection . . .

Randy: You literally just described me as an adult.

Mom: And when you were a teen, we would go to the mall and girls with short-shorts and big boobs would walk past and I would watch to see if you turned your head to look. Never once did I see that happen.

Randy: Maybe I was just classy.

Mom: No, you were just gay. I remember when you were eighteen and you told me you were gay and I said, "Right. Now please consider going to college. Oh, and condoms, Randy."

Randy: Well, one out of two ain't bad. My father pretended to be genuinely shocked. How the fuck was that possible? Didn't he live in our house?

Mom: Oh, please. He didn't know what the hell was going on. I think I could have brought another man into the marriage bed and he wouldn't have noticed. He was the ultimate narcissist.

Randy: Well, I've already told everyone that my father was basically Donald Trump. Do you concur?

Mom: I do concur. In fairness, however, your father had better hair.

Randy: How do you explain marrying him/Donald Trump?

Mom: Your father was a real charmer. Very handsome and talented. Beautiful voice, an entertainer. And of course, there was that little misunderstanding we had.

Randy: What was that?

Mom: He thought I had money and I thought he had money. We were both wrong, but by then, we were already married.

Randy: Two gold diggers. Great. What do you remember most about my relationship with him?

Mom: Oh god, the horrific tension in the room whenever you were both together. Most nights, you ate dinner in your room just to avoid his sour expressions. It was an ulcer-inducing time.

Randy: I feel like it wasn't always like that from the beginning. . . .

Mom: No, this all began when you hit puberty, because up until that time, you two had a pretty decent relationship. He would take you to his band rehearsals, teach you songs . . . Your big mistake was growing up and becoming a threat to

him. He started to see you as competition and he
just couldn't deal with that.

Randy: That's a real healthy dynamic for a parent
and child. What made you finally divorce him?

Mom: When Nanny died, I looked into her coffin
and realized that chronologically I was next up.
I was not going to spend one more day miserable.
Life's short, kiddo!

Randy: I was famously antisocial as a kid. What
did you make of all my isolating?

Mom: I think that happened at puberty, as well.
You had lots of little friends as a small child.
And you had lots of friends as a teenager, but
you were not a joiner. Your friends would get
together on the weekend to do things, and you
would decline to join. Not always but certainly
enough that I remember it happening all these
years later.

Randy: Well, I spent most weekends with Nanny
well into my teens. Why do you think she and I
had such a special bond?

Mom: Your Nanny provided you with the uncondi-
tional love that you deserved and did not necessarily get at home. She adored you. She was

the one who picked you up after school every day because I had to work. I think grandparents are notoriously nicer to their grandchildren than their own children in general. They can spoil the hell out of them because they get to give them back at the end of the day, and don't have to be responsible for how the little brats turn out. I also think that my very close relationship with her helped to cement your relationship with her. She was there from the moment of your birth. Literally. I was knocked out cold from anesthesia after a C-section, and she got to see you and hold you before I was even awake. She was the first person you laid eyes on out of the womb, not counting Dr. Lippert.

Randy: Is that who delivered me?

Mom: Yeah.

Randy: Shout-out to Dr. Lippert. Love your work.

Mom: He was the one who first confirmed your poor sense of direction when, days before my due date, he told me you were heading in the wrong direction and would never find your way out without help. How you get around Manhattan now continues to amaze me.

Randy: It's not my fault. Do you know how hard it is to get an Uber in your uterus?

Mom: That's funny.

Randy: I know. Speaking of . . . how would you describe our sense of humor? Cynical? Sardonic? Sarcastic? Asshole-ish?

Mom: Yes, all of the above.

Randy: I feel like so much of our humor is fueled by anger. Why is that?

Mom: Because we're angry all the time, dammit!

Randy: We somehow find ways to laugh in the face of tragedy, or at serious topics others might consider inappropriate for comedy. What's the deal with that. . . . Are we just psychopaths?

Mom: Obviously. I am constantly getting called out by my friends as being inappropriate. It's a gift.

Randy: Were you surprised when I picked up and moved back to New York?

Mom: Actually, the way I remember it is that you were surprised. When we found out you had an opportunity to stay at your friend Courtney's aunt's place and try your luck in New York, I packed you up, drove you to the airport, and dropped you on your ass at the gate. I could not wait to get rid of you.

Randy: Oh that's real nice.

Mom: You were so miserable by that time. I really didn't think there was anything else for you but to leave and start your real life. And you never came back.

Randy: How proud were you when I landed my job at Hooters?

Mom: Oh, it was the highlight of my life as a mother.

Randy: Be honest . . . there were a few years there when you didn't know if I'd make it in New York, right?

Mom: When I think about the obstacles you had to overcome to stay there, sleeping on people's couches, not having a career, not having a sense of direction . . .

Randy: Okay, we covered my shitty sense of direction already . . .

Mom: I don't remember ever thinking you'd be back in South Florida ever again. That's how miserable I knew you were at home. Plus, we had changed the locks by then.

Randy: When did you finally know I'd be okay? Or are you still on the fence?

Mom: I remember when you filled Birdland with people who came to see you and who were coming over to me saying they had traveled from other states to see you perform, that was a hint to me you were on the right track. I have always known you were talented, but also that you are a very nice person. In grade school you got an award for helping a little girl find her way to her class. You're a mensch.

Randy: Yeah, fuck the Emmy. I'm a one-time "helped a little girl find her class" award winner.

Mom: Oh, shut up. People seem to gravitate to you. They like you. They really, really like you.

Randy: Okay, Sally Field. I feel like song parodies have always indirectly been a part of my life. Weren't you always singing random song parodies around the house?

Mom: You know, I grew up in the town where one of the writers of *Mad* magazine lived. He even went to my high school and used my school in many of the skits in the magazine. *Mad* was famous for parodies. They put out a record of songs with titles like "Sam and Janet Evening" to the tune of "Some Enchanted Evening," and others that escape my aging brain right now.

Randy: This is all starting to make sense now.

Mom: And I grew up in a house that had all of Allan Sherman's comedy albums. He was a king of parody. We also had all the great Jewish comics' albums—Myron Cohen, Jackie Mason. So my brain always turns to parody as a default.

Randy: What's been your favorite part of these last five crazy years of my career? Was it the Dyson vacuum cleaner I bought you for Hanukkah last year, or the fact that I know Alan Cumming?

Mom: Alan Cumming. And if you don't introduce me to him already, I'm gonna murder you.

Randy: All in good time, my little pretty. Can you believe we're actually friends with Carol Burnett now? You're welcome, by the way.

Mom: This is a big one. She is such a wonderful, kind, and lovely human being. We keep in touch via email, and she even sent me her boxed set of every single Carol Burnett episode. She has been extremely supportive of you and let's face it, when Carol Burnett tells you that you're funny, you're funny.

Randy: You've become very famous yourself. What's been your most memorable encounter with a fan?

Mom: Wow, there have been so many. People are always thanking me for giving birth to you. How do I even answer that?

Randy: I hope it's not by telling them that I couldn't find my way out of your vagina because I have no sense of direction.

Mom: No, I don't say that.

Randy: Thank god. Well, Stephen Sondheim had the honor of sitting next to you at my first show at the Beacon Theatre. Tell us everything.

Mom: This was a real surprise for me. Your tour manager kept telling me to make sure I was sitting in seat number 112 . . . not to sit anywhere else but 112. When I got to the theater, I found seat 112, looked at the gentleman on my right, and realized it was Stephen Sondheim! We had met before, I believe in 2009. When you took me to that Tony Awards after-party for *Company*. We both had poodles at the time, so we talked about poodles—

Randy: Yeah, yeah, back to me. What did he think of my show?

Mom: Well, the best part of sitting with him was watching his reactions. He was guffawing and raising his hands in the air to clap for you and just totally enjoying himself. During the Q&A, a fan asked what were your favorite shows and, of course, you named one of his, not knowing that he was in the audience, and he really got a kick out of that. So, I guess that's really my most memorable encounter with a fan.

Randy: Do you still have the pack of Tic Tacs Anthony Anderson borrowed from you at the Emmys?

Mom: It's in the safe.

Randy: Have you spoken to Josh Gad's mother recently?

Mom: She and I go back to when you two were kids at the Hollywood Playhouse. We keep in touch and talk on the phone from time to time. So, last week she told me one of her friends found out that she knew me—which is apparently a big deal these days—and got so excited! She couldn't wait to tell me this! I mean, here is the mother of a major successful star of Broadway and movies and television telling me how great *my* kid is!

Randy: Well, why do you have to say it like that?

Mom: You know what I mean. I love that woman.

Randy: Lots of eligible bachelors will likely want to date me once this book hits *The New York Times* Best Seller list. What are you looking for in a suitor for me?

Mom: I would like you to find a man who would, of course, love you but also not be intimidated by your success. Someone who gets you. Someone who is his own man with his own life. The best relationships I know are the ones where each partner can function independently but also be a full partner for life. Someone who makes you happy and makes you laugh. A sense of humor is hugely important. And a sense of direction would be very helpful.

Randy: Oh god, moving on. When are you gonna start dating? Are you still on that app?

Mom: I tried that "our time is almost up" app. I paid my money, spent an hour looking at people I wouldn't want to even share an Uber with, called customer service and told the nice young man I wanted my money back, that I had decided to get a dog instead. So, no, not on the app. But if the right poodle came along . . .

Randy: How many years do you think we have left before we fully become *Grey Gardens*?

Mom: I'd say five years, tops.

Randy: I'd say you're being generous. Well, anyway, looks like we're out of time for now.

Mom: Good, 'cause I'm late for book club already.

Randy: Let's hear it for my mom, ladies and gentlemen!

(APPLAUSE)

Mom: This was very enjoyable and I will expect royalties.

Randy: Don't push it, mother darling. We'll be right back after these commercial messages!

23

What Are You Gonna Do?

"What are you gonna do, Randy? What are you gonna do?" Of all the questions I've gotten over the last several years, that's probably the one I've heard the most (aside from, "Is that your real name?" and "Why are you texting my husband in the middle of the night?").

To be honest, it's a question that's always made me cringe a little. Of course, a lot of the reasons for that are tied up in my own mishegas. As you've just read in this book, I was a late bloomer. I didn't find my real path until my midthirties. Like my mom always said, I was never one to crawl before I walked. Still, that never stopped her and other family members from asking some form of the question any chance they got: "What are you gonna do with yourself? What are you gonna do if your plan doesn't work out? When are you gonna settle on a career? What do you wanna be when you grow up?"

Though it seemed I'd finally figured some of that stuff out, I was still getting asked the question. Except the latest version, which had been coming from strangers almost every day since the 2016 election, was, "What are you gonna do when Trump is out of office?" The question wasn't exclusive to me, of course. It was being asked of everyone doing Trump jokes (as if there'd been any other kind for four years) from writers on *SNL* and *The Daily Show* to late-night hosts like Stephen Colbert. It always seemed so shortsighted to me to assume that all comedians would become hairdressers after Trump left the White House.

Frankly, I find the insinuation that I or any respectable comedian would need to rely on a Donald Trump or any one public figure to create solid comedy wildly offensive. I'll have you know that my post-Trump comedy game is stronger than ever. In fact, here are just a few rough samples of topical jokes randomly selected from my notes app that I happen to be working on right now:

What's up with Uber drivers rating me? I mean, I'm the paying customer and this guy whose only known job qualification is owning a little cardboard tree that smells like coconut is determining my grade point average? What's next? Actors reviewing how we watch their movies? Pizza delivery boys updating our credit scores?

That one's still not exactly where I want it yet. How about this one?

Where does the milk in almond milk actually come from? I mean, do almonds even have nipples?

And hey, what's the deal with flaxseeds . . . ?

Anyway, maybe those still need some workshopping. The point is, no one man defines me, honey! In fact, no individual target defines any comedian or satirist. Case closed.

Bad jokes aside, on a more personal level, the constant suggestion that I would forever be defined by Donald Trump, of all people, was a direct callback to my father—the Donald Trump clone of all fathers—standing in that den in South Florida, telling teenage me that any of my accomplishments in life were actually his. I almost had to laugh at the irony. It was almost like he was punking me from beyond the grave.

In November of 2020, Trump lost the election. (Sorry . . . "allegedly.") I bid him farewell with a *Rent* parody called "Seasons of Trump," in which I recapped all of the atrocities of his four years in office. Anthony Rapp from the original Broadway cast of *Rent* tweeted the video, saying that Jonathan Larson would be proud of me. Doesn't get better than that.

As I suspected, Trump's departure created no shortage of material for satire. When Biden became president, I continued to make my song parody videos, singing mostly about COVID-19, the batshit villains in the GOP, and other such existential threats to humanity. (As long as there's misery and destruction in the world, I'll be open for business.)

In February of 2021, a new GOP breakout star suddenly hijacked the headlines. Marjorie Taylor Greene, a recently elected congresswoman representing Georgia's Fourteenth Congressional District, was in hot water because of—what else—old tweets. The resurfaced posts and videos exposed Greene's promotion of extreme right-wing conspiracy theories and many of QAnon's greatest hits—e.g., 9/11 was an inside job, the Sandy Hook and Parkland shootings were staged, Donald Trump was elected by Jesus to save children from being eaten by pedophile lizard people living in the dungeon of Hillary Clinton's pizza parlor. . . . (Don't fact-check me on that last one . . . I can't keep up with this shit.) She was unapologetically bigoted, wildly controversial, and, to put it in medical terms, wacky as fuck. In short, she was the stuff Randy Rainbow videos are made of!

One of her most talked about and anti-Semitic conspiracy theories involved Jewish-funded lasers beaming down on California from outer space, causing what normal earthlings would consider natural wildfires, in order to make room for high-speed rail projects. #JewishSpaceLasers soon began trending on Twitter, and while most normal earthlings were busy remarking on the absurd offensiveness of her dangerous rhetoric and demanding her removal from office, I had costume choices to make. I suddenly remembered a children's astronaut costume that Amazon had mistakenly shipped me along with a wig order I'd placed the previous October. I always felt bad thinking of the poor little kid whose Halloween plans had no doubt already gone to hell in a handbasket thanks to Covid, now missing their costume to boot. But all that compassion flew out the window as I ran to my studio and pulled the shiny plastic Party City package from the dark, dusty corner of my prop closet. (Tough break, kid!) The astronaut suit part barely slid past my dainty wrist, but the space helmet fit like a glove! It was what we in the Jewish Space Laser community might call *bashert*. (The Space Laser gentiles in the audience might need to google that.)

Now that wardrobe was underway, I needed to choose a song for MTG. The "green" angle is what first struck me, and like any basic, ultragay show tune parodist worth his glitter, I thought, "Wicked!" No, there was nothing for Marjorie there. What about "Somewhere That's Green" from *Little Shop of Horrors*? Perhaps. I was vacuuming my apartment in the rainbow rhinestone stilettos the fabulous Ana Navarro had sent me as a Pride gift one year. In the interest of full transparency, and at the risk of disappointing you, I do not usually vacuum in heels. I was just being cute for an Instagram post. My Streisand Spotify was playing in the background and like a divine intervention from my lord and savior, Barbra herself, "Evergreen" shuffled on.

"Perfect!" I thought. "What better way to take on a radical anti-Semitic lunatic than with an Academy Award–winning Barbra Streisand love ballad?!"

I got to work, and posted the video thirty-six hours later. It was a hit with almost six million views in its first day. Even the legendary Paul Williams, who wrote the lyrics to the original song, sent his enthusiastic blessing. It was my first video under a new presidential administration, and I'd be lying if I said I didn't feel the tiniest twinge of vindication, having been trolled for so long by all those skeptics who assumed I'd turn into a pumpkin the second Trump left office. It felt like I was waking up at the end of the movie *Groundhog Day* and Andie MacDowell was still in bed next to me.

● ● ● ● ●

Around this time, headlines were piling up with sexual assault allegations against Andrew Cuomo. My "Andy!" video was being posted all over Twitter by his haters and mine in an effort to, I suppose, shame me and anyone who'd praised him in 2020. It was Christmas for the trolls. My phone started blowing up with calls, emails, and text messages from reporters at the *New York Post*, *The Daily Beast*, even *The New York Times* wanting—in some cases demanding—my comments.

"What do you have to say for yourself now, Cuomosexual???"

"Um, are you referring to the song parody from the musical *Grease* I sang a year and a half ago while dressed as a Pink Lady . . . ? No comment."

They were essentially interrogating a cartoon character, which, as always, seemed odd to me. In case anyone is genuinely interested in what I, the actual person, felt about the downfall of Andrew Cuomo (and it seems many are), I was disappointed. I appreciated his leadership (flawed though it may have been) during a horrifying and unprecedented time. I don't regret making my video about him because, at the time, it brought a little musical levity to people when they needed it most, and for me that's always a win. The implication that my silly parody from a year prior to the allegations that ultimately led to his resignation was or is in any way an endorsement or condonation of sexual harassment is gross and disingenuous. Some asked during that time why I didn't aim my comedy at the headline. To be honest, it just wasn't something I felt like singing about, and luckily I've never been obligated to. I'm not a journalist. I work for myself and I get to do whatever I feel like doing. It's fucking fabulous. . . . I recommend it.

· · · · ·

That spring, I got an email from my longtime friend, and concert director to Barbra Streisand, Richard Jay-Alexander. He asked if I'd be available to jump on a call with him and Barbra's legendary team, producer Jay Landers and Marty Erlichman—the man who discovered Barbra and had been her manager for over fifty years. It just so happened I was available to take the call.

They told me they had seen my Marjorie Taylor "Evergreen" parody, and that Barbra herself loved it. (OMFG@!@#$%@#!!&#!!!!!!!!!) They asked if I'd be willing to create a video celebrating the release of her upcoming new album, *Release Me 2*, the second installment in her compilation series of previously unreleased recordings from her personal vault (or as I call it, her Oy Ge-Vault). Jay suggested a parody version of "I'm the Greatest Star" from *Funny Girl*. Well, twist *my* arm! I told them how honored I was to be asked and gratefully accepted the assignment before hanging up and getting to work. This was the collaboration I'd been dreaming of my whole life. I couldn't let my Barbra down!

I wrote the lyrics and then called an emergency meeting with my music director and producer. We worked out a special music arrangement of the song and I had them assemble the best Broadway musicians they could find to record the track. While they got busy doing that, I jumped online and cobbled together the finest Fanny Brice knockoff costume money could buy on Amazon Prime. (It was $47.95.)

A few weeks later, the song was recorded and the video was wrapped. Per the master plan carefully strategized by Sony Music and Barbra's personal team, I posted my Barbra Streisand appreciation song parody. Less than a half hour later . . . on June 25th at 9:38 A.M. Eastern, a tweet . . . from Barbra . . .

Dear Randy—

Your musical and visual creativity are like buttah!

With my thanks and warm regards.
B.

Oh my god, she typed my name. I knew from past interviews she'd done that she personally does all her own tweeting, and couldn't wrap my brain around the fact that Barbra Joan Streisand used her magnificent, elegant, legendary, perfectly manicured, French-tipped fingernails to type my name. I didn't know what to do with all my emotions. I lit a Bath & Body Works candle and recited the haftarah from my bar mitzvah.

I called my mother immediately. "Mom! Barbra responded to my video!"

"WHAAAAAAT???" she shrieked, emitting a high-pitched sound so beyond the range of normal human frequency that only other Jewish mothers in the surrounding area could hear it.

"She liked the video . . . she retweeted it . . . and she said I'm like butter . . ." I was talking so fast, my mouth couldn't keep up with my words. My mother was the one who first introduced me to Barbra all those years ago, and loved her so much herself. I was so excited for us to share this special moment. I read her the tweet verbatim. "Mom! Can you believe it??? Barbra!"

"I don't know," said my mother, pausing to evaluate what I'd just told her. "She couldn't be bothered to pick up the phone?"

• • • • •

Eh . . . What are you gonna do?

24

Me, My Selfie & iPhone

I still wasn't wearing pants when I attended the 73rd Primetime Emmy Awards in September of 2021. I had been nominated for a third time, sharing the category with a segment from *Late Night with Seth Meyers*, Stephen Colbert's animated *Tooning Out the News*, *Reno 911!*, and James Corden's *Carpool Karaoke*. After eighteen months at home, I was finally getting ready to tour again. Because of my rehearsal schedule, I couldn't fly out to L.A. for the ceremony, so I opted to attend virtually from home, via Zoom.

The opening montage started playing on the giant LEDs in the Microsoft Theater, and as clips of Oprah, Stephen Colbert, *South Park*, and others flashed on the screen, one flashed of me (singing a song to Senator Josh Hawley of Missouri, no less). Bernadette Peters, ravishing as always, took the stage to announce my category, which seemed too dreamy to be true and a sure sign of good luck. But for the third year in a row, I lost to *Carpool Karaoke*. I sent a tweet urging everyone to storm the U.S. Capitol, but no one followed my instructions. (And you guys call yourselves fans. . . .) I was alone in my living room, essentially where it all began. Everything was as it always had been, and yet so much had changed.

· · · · ·

I don't know how any of this happened. I left my parents' house almost twenty years ago, trying to find my way over the rainbow. Maybe the smarter thing would have been to follow my friends to college, and show up at the cattle calls like I was supposed to. I don't think I was brave or confident enough to take a more conventional path. But maybe the one I ended up carving for myself took even more courage than I thought. I followed my heart to Manhattan and built myself a one-of-a-kind hot-air balloon (Scotch Tape included) . . . I made my own Ruby Slippers (and sold them on Etsy) . . . I even banged a few flying monkeys (refer to chapter 9). Then, just when I thought I'd lost my way, a great big ugly orange cyclone swept me up and took me on a crazy, wild ride around the world. And yet somehow, I've never left my own backyard.

It's been a year and a half since the world stopped, and in that time so many of the people I met along the yellow brick road that led me here (and then I swear that's the last *Wizard of Oz* reference for this chapter) circled back into my life. The producer whose phones I answered and whose coffee I made almost fifteen years ago recently called to say he would love to discuss producing a one-man show for me on Broadway. (To quote Elaine Stritch: "If that's not a Cinderella story, I'll eat one.") My friend Josh Gad and I finally reconnected and started working together on a new project. Sean Hayes offered to produce a podcast for me with his production company Hazy Mills, which we'll start work on soon. I just finished recording my first full-length solo album. Josh and Sean both sang a song with me in it (our own rendition

of "You Gotta Have a Gimmick" from *Gypsy* . . . Can you even???).
Also duetting with me on the album . . . my beloved Tituss Burgess,
and (are you sitting down?) Bernadette freakin' Peters. As I write this
now, I'm finally preparing to embark on my brand-new tour . . . "The
Pink Glasses Tour," complete with an original title song (a tribute to my
Nanny) written by Alan Menken and yours truly.

Oh, I also wrote a book! (I guess you already figured that out by
now.) I hope you liked it. If not, go easy, would ya? It's my first time. I
had a number of reasons for wanting to chronicle a few of my adventures so far. For one (as I'm sure many of you can relate), the last couple
of years threw me into a bit of an existential crisis, and I wanted to take
stock. I guess I wanted to celebrate some of the good and clear up some
of the misunderstood. I wanted to say goodbye to my cat. I wanted to
say thank you to the women in my life who helped shape me, and to
close a few chapters on some of the men with whom my relationships
have been slightly more complicated (Mel Gibson included). I also
wanted to apologize to Jimmy Kimmel and Zachary Levi.

Most importantly, I think I wanted to finally introduce myself. So
many of you have been so generous in sharing your personal stories
with me over the years. I wanted to return the favor and let you know
a little bit about the person behind the persona. Of course, I wasn't
able to squeeze everything into my first memoir. So before I let you go,
here—in no particular order—are a few miscellaneous facts about me
I may have left out:

1. I hate the summer.

2. I love coffee ice cream.

3. My first job was at Dairy Queen.

4. My first car was a silver 1986 Buick Century that I named Tiffany after the 1980s pop star.

5. My second car was an electric-blue 1999 Kia Sephia that I named Britney after Britney Spears because I'm awesome.

6. I have extremely soft hands. Like, abnormally soft.

7. I got a new cat! Her name is Tippi. She's a silver Chinchilla Persian and she is gorgeous and a riot and very polite. Her original name was Sweeney (as in Sweeney Todd) because we thought she was a boy kitten until her second trip to the vet. It only took a couple of days to adjust to her new pronouns, and it wasn't a big deal at all.

So now you've learned a few things about me. Hell, even *I've* learned a few things about me while writing this book. For one, I'm finally ready to say: My name is Randy Rainbow (yes, really) and I'm a hard-core, out-and-proud, full-blown introvert!!! (Sorry, that was kind of loud.) I'm no longer ashamed to admit it. I deeply love being alone, and it's served me well. I've spent a lot of time throughout the years locked in my room, hiding from scary fathers, global pandemics, and sometimes just life itself. Sure, it's been lonely at times, but certainly not without its perks. It's where I discovered myself and ultimately the power to express and create in ways I never thought I could. Having said that, the past eighteen months have also taught me just how much I love people (some of them, anyway). As exhausting as they can be, I thrive on other people. I need them, dammit. In fact, it's my belief that people who need people are the luckiest people in the . . . fine, I didn't write that either.

My antisocial tendencies have gotten me in a lot of trouble with many of my friends over the years, so allow me to take this opportunity to apologize to those people for all the calls and text messages I never returned, and all the dinner plans I canceled at the last minute. It isn't that I didn't want to spend time with you (well, for *some* of you that was the reason . . .). It's just that I was busy writing, stewing, singing, sulking, reflecting, recharging, bingeing, planning, filming, worrying, thinking, pacing, creating. Please refer to this passage as often as is necessary (because you know I'm never calling you back) and believe me when I tell you, it's not you, babe . . . it's me.

* * * * *

Thank you again for coming to my book. Don't forget to tip your waiter, watch your step as you exit, and remember: Life sucks sometimes. Find the thing that brings you joy and wear it proudly like a pair of ridiculous Pink Glasses. Laugh at everything—even at funerals (within reason), and if the mood strikes you, don't be afraid to burst into song now and again. Be weird, and above all, resist the urge to let others define you . . . don't do them the honor. For god's sake, get off social media every once in a while (by the way, follow me @RandyRainbow on all platforms), and spend some quality time with you. Go on . . . play with yourself.

* * * * *

All right, now get the hell outta here . . . I need some me time.

Acknowledgments

I would like to thank my mother, Gwen, for nurturing me every step of the way, for never discouraging me from wearing pajama bottoms on my head, for always being my biggest fan and supporter through the best and worst, and for helping me remember it all for this book. I'm so grateful to have been paired with an editor as divine as Michael Flamini, who brilliantly guarded and guided me, and more importantly, got all of my musical theatre references. Thank you to everyone at St. Martin's Press for welcoming me to their family. (Here's to many more, I hope!) Bravo and thanks to my literary agent, Anthony Mattero, for having the wisdom to choose such a perfect team for me, and for holding my hand through this process. Thank you to Ari Levin, Matt Blake, Jillian Doyle, and everyone at CAA for helping to make this dream, and so many more, come true. Thank you to Andy Levitt (and his mother) and everyone at Live Nation for their incredible generosity and support through the years. I'd be remiss not to acknowledge the long list of friends, family, teachers, and collaborators that includes (but is certainly not limited to) Stephen Sondheim, Carol Burnett, Victoria Varela, Ryan Raftery, Ben Davis, Paul Pecorino, Tituss Burgess, Frank DiLella, Heather Ricks, Julie James, Mark MacKillop, Victor J. Wisehart, Evyan Wagner, Matt Gilhooly, Kelly Hobby, Benjamin Lynn, Sami Rudnick-Hoover, Vanessa Baker, Laurie Cohen ("other mother"), John Retsios, Jeff Romley, Tippi, Mushi, Courtney Gilbert, Zach Taylor, Richard Jay-Alexander, Tanase Popa, Jesse Kissel, Michael J. Moritz, Jr., James Michael, Dawn Sclafani, Marc Shaiman, Alan Menken, Rosie O'Donnell, Melissa Gilbert and Tim Busfield, Josh Gad, Sean Hayes, Bernadette Peters, Patti Fucking LuPone, Lorna Luft, Pamela Adlon, Robert Fried, Karen Kowgios, David Goldman, Frank Galgano, Jim Caruso, Rich Super, Judy Gold, Joe Watson, Tania Senewiratne, Jason Pelusio, Anthony Taccetta, the Frankels (Josh, Janis, Rob, Jaymee, Lianne, Andy), and Gerard Salvador (my "Suz"), who all played a significant role in my story so far. To Bob Saget (we never got to sing our duet, but I'll always cherish our lovely connection and be grateful for his support). Thank you to my longtime fans and followers for taking this wild ride with me and for being so generous with your love and gratitude. . . . You have no idea how mutual it is. Finally, eternal love and thanks to my dearly departed Nanny, Irene Frankel. Every time joy and laughter fill my heart, I see your face.